Numerology

Master and Design Your Perfect Life by Combining Numbers, Astrology, and Tarot to Unlock Your Happiness and Destiny

(Learn Relationships and Dating Compatibility Using Numerology)

Gary Buchanan

Published by Rob Miles

© **Gary Buchanan**

All Rights Reserved

Numerology: Master and Design Your Perfect Life by Combining Numbers, Astrology, and Tarot to Unlock Your Happiness and Destiny (Learn Relationships and Dating Compatibility Using Numerology)

ISBN 978-1-989990-39-1

All rights reserved. No part of this guide may be reproduced in any form without permission in writing from the publisher except in the case of brief quotations embodied in critical articles or reviews.

Legal & Disclaimer

The information contained in this book is not designed to replace or take the place of any form of medicine or professional medical advice. The information in this book has been provided for educational and entertainment purposes only.

The information contained in this book has been compiled from sources deemed reliable, and it is accurate to the best of the Author's knowledge; however, the Author cannot guarantee its accuracy and validity and cannot be held liable for any errors or omissions. Changes are periodically made to this book. You must consult your doctor or get professional medical advice before using any of the suggested remedies, techniques, or information in this book.

Upon using the information contained in this book, you agree to hold harmless the Author from and against any damages, costs, and expenses, including any legal fees potentially resulting from the application of any of the information provided by this guide. This disclaimer applies to any damages or injury caused by the use and application, whether directly or indirectly, of any advice or information presented, whether for breach of contract, tort, negligence, personal injury, criminal intent, or under any other cause of action.

You agree to accept all risks of using the information presented inside this book. You need to consult a professional medical practitioner in order to ensure you are both able and healthy enough to participate in this program.

Table of Contents

INTRODUCTION 1

CHAPTER 1 : THE PERSONALITY NUMBERS 3

CHAPTER 2: BASIC ELEMENTS OF NUMEROLOGY 20

CHAPTER 3: THE HISTORY OF NUMEROLOGY 32

CHAPTER 4: THE ASTROLOGICAL IDEA 38

CHAPTER 5: A MISUNDERSTOOD ART FORM 49

CHAPTER 6: BASIC UNDERSTANDING TOWARD NUMEROLOGY? 52

CHAPTER 7: HOW TO OUTLINE YOUR NUMEROLOGY LIFE PROFILE 59

CHAPTER 8: MEANING OF EACH NUMBER 76

CHAPTER 9: JUPITER (NUMBER – 3) 83

CHAPTER 10: CLEAR AS CRYSTAL; CRYSTAL HEALING FACTS 91

CHAPTER 11: NUMEROLOGY POSITIONS, PATTERNS, AND FORMULAS 108

CHAPTER 12: THE MAGICIAN 121

CHAPTER 13: THE VEDIC INFLUENCE ON NUMBERS 135

CHAPTER 14: YOUR SOCIAL ATTRIBUTES 140

CHAPTER 15: THE BASIC NUMEROLOGY CHART 145

CHAPTER 16: KARMIC DEBT NUMBERS (KDN) : 150

CHAPTER 17: ENTREPRENEUR, ACCOUNTANT, BOSS, MANAGER, PLANNER HEART OF THE ACCOUNTANT 163

CHAPTER 18: MATURITY NUMBER 178

CONCLUSION 184

Introduction

Have you ever thought about numbers and the influence they can have on your life? The eccentric fact is that you can use numbers to reveal many things including your whole persona; your character, what motivates you, your talents, and purpose in life. With the help of numerology experts, numbers can also be used to plan activities and major changes in your life such as the career you should follow and the right time to change jobs, invest, travel, relocate, marry, and even the names you will give your future babies, if any.

The initial question that may come to your mind when you are exposed to this compelling truth is how and why these numbers work. Well, wonder no more for this book will provide a deep insight into the amazing art of numerology and try to answer most, if not all your burning questions.

Chapter 1 : The Personality Numbers

THE PERSONALITY PROFILE

In numerology, a profile of personality consists of seven numbers of personalities making a person who they are. Your ability to "mix" each of these seven numbers together is the key to an accurate reading.

Each of the seven pieces plays a unique part of their own, but it is the mixture of all seven parts that complete the puzzle. If a part of the numerology puzzle is absent, the tale of an individual is incomplete, so you need to construct an accurate summary of your character and existence in each of the seven parts.

This takes practice, persistence, and effort to put all the numbers together. However, you will be reading a numerology chart like a pro once you get the hang of it.

The seven Personality Numbers are:

The Life Path Number

The Destiny Number

The Soul Number

The Personality Number

The Maturity Number

The Current Name Number

The Birth Day Number

These figures are determined from the full, original name of the birth certificate, the date of birth, and the latest names used today.

THE LIFE PATH NUMBER

Of the seven Personality Numbers, the most significant of all is the Life Path Number. It gives you the most information about your character and the type of life you are going to live.

Your Life Path Number shows the meaning of your life and the path you have chosen to follow in this lifetime. It shows the type of life experiences that you will encounter and the lessons that you will learn along the way.

The Ruling Number, the Birth Number, the Birth Path, or the Birth Force Number is also regarded as the Life Path Number. It is named the Destiny Number of Chaldean numerology.

HOW TO CALCULATE THE LIFE PATH NUMBER

Your Life Path Number is determined by putting together all the numbers in your date of birth. There are three ways to do this; however, "adding across" and "reducing down" are the two most commonly used methods. No method is right or wrong—they're just different. The form chosen is just a matter of personal preference.

ADDING ACROSS

This is how to measure a Life Path Number by putting all the numbers in your birth date together by moving them across:

Step 1: Make sure you're adding the entire birth year—not just 69, for instance, in 1969.

Use the date of birth as an example on 11 October 1969 (10–11–1969): 1+ 0 + 1 + 1 + 1 + 9 + 6 + 9= 28

Step 2: Try to put any double-digit numbers together until you get a single-digit Life Path number between 1 and 9 unless it is 11, 22, and 33, which will then be 11/2, 22/4, and 33/6.

2 + 8= 10

1+ 0= 1 Life Path Number

Finally, let's see what happens when we get 33, as with the date of birth on January 8, 1968 (1-8-1968)

1+ 8 + 1 + 9 + 6 + 8= 33 Life Path Number.

Since we do not add 11, 22, or 33 together, this would be a 33/6 Life Path Number.

REDUCING DOWN

Let's look now at the reduction-down process. This is how a Life Path Number can be determined by reducing:

Step 1: Reduce the birth date's month, day, and year numbers to three single-digit numbers unless they are 11 and 22. (If they total 11 or 22, don't reduce them down keep them as 11 or 22).

Let's use the birth date, December 11, 1969 (12–11–1969), as an example:

1+2 / 11 / 1+9+6+9 = 25

3112+5

Step 2: Add together the single figures (or 11 and 22, if applicable) and continue to add any double-digit numbers until you get a single-digit Life Path number between 1 and 9. If a Life Path Number is 11, 22, or 33, it will not be limited to 2, 4, or 6. This stays 11, 22, and 33 and becomes a Life Path Number of 11/2, 22/4, and 33/6.

3+11+7 = 21

2+1 = 3 life Path number

Now let's see what happens with the birth date January 8, 1968 (1-8-1968) that previously gave us a 33/6 Life Path

1 / 8 / 1+9+6+8 = 24

1 / 8 2+4 =6

1+8+6 = 15

1+5 = 6 life Path number

As you can see, we are reduced to 15 (before a reduction-down to a 6 Life Path Number) by the reduction-down method and 33 by the adding-across process. So how do we know the correct method? One of numerology's most confusing things is that we don't. All that is known is that most qualified numerologists agree that the reduction-down process is the most reliable of all when deciding a real 11/2, 22/4, or 33/6 Master Number.

THE DESTINY NUMBER

The Destiny Number is your numerology chart's second most significant number. It is also known as the Title or Expression

Number and is derived from the full, original name of the birth certificate. This number reveals what you are meant to do and who you are meant to become in this lifetime. It shows skills that already reside within you and must be used throughout this lifetime. This is the number to consider when choosing a career along with the Life Path Number.

The total, original name of the birth certificate is used to determine the Destiny Number irrespective of whether or not you are still using the name—and whether or not you have been adopted and changed your name through marriage or another way. Even if you only had that name for the birth certificate for one day, and even if that name for the birth certificate was simply "Baby," that is the name to use.

HOW TO CALCULATE THE DESTINY NUMBER

1	2	3	4	5	6	7	8	9

A	B	C	D	e	F	G	H	I
J	K	l	m	n	o	P	Q	R
S	T	U	V	W	X	y	Z	

Step 1: Write the complete, initial birth certificate name and add the appropriate numbers to each letter using the Western Pythagorean letters-and-numbers map above.

Please note that a hyphenated or compound last name is deemed to be one name, and names like Junior (Jr.) or Senior (Sr.) are not included in the equation. You only need to measure your first and last name if you don't have a middle name. If you have several middle names, each middle name has to be determined individually.

Make sure you leave plenty of space between each letter, so you don't lose out on a count.

For instance, let's use the name Mary Ann Smith:

MARY ANN SMITH

<u>4+1+9+7 1+5+5 1+4+9+2+8</u>

Step 2: To add individual numbers, insert each title separately.

MARY ANN SMITH

<u>4+1+9+7 1+5+5 1+4+9+2+8</u>

21   11   24

Step 3: To create single-number totals, add double-digit totals together unless the total is 11, 22, or 33. (If they don't reduce a total of 11, 22, or 33 – keep them as 11, 22, or 33).

MARY ANN   SMITH

<u>4+1+9+7</u> <u>1+5+5</u> <u>1+4+9+2+8</u>

 21   11   24

<u>2+1</u>   <u>11</u>   <u>2+4</u>

  3   11   6

Step 4: Add the individual figures together (or 11, 22, and 33 if applicable) and attach any double-digit numbers together until a single-digit Destiny Number between 1

11

and 9 is gotten. If a Destiny Number is 11, 22, or 33, it will not be limited to 2, 4, or 6. It remains 11, 22, or 33 and becomes a Destiny Number of 11/2, 22/4, or 33/6.

3+11+6 = 20

2+0 = 2 Destiny number

You will use this very same method to determine the Current Name Number, Business Name Number, and any other naming details, and I recommend you bookmark this page for future reference. Keep these equations handy as you will need to return to them to calculate the Karmic Lesson Numbers.

THE SOUL NUMBER

The Soul Number is the third most important number in your numerology chart and is also known as the Soul's Urge, Soul's Desire, or Heart's Desire. To feel complete, it reveals what your soul needs (and wants) you to be. In other terms, if you were to follow this number's positive traits, your soul would feel satisfied and content.

The soul number in your birth certificate name is calculated from the vowels.

HOW TO CALCULATE THE SOUL NUMBER

Step 1: Add the numbers in your birth certificate name that match the vowels

Step 2: To create specific numbers, insert every title separately. To create single-number totals, add double-digit totals together (unless they total 11, 22, or 33 that remain 11, 22, or 33).

M A RA N NS M I T H

  y

1 7 1   9

1 + 7 1   9

  8

Step 3: Add the single figures together (or 11, 22, and 33 if applicable) and continue to add any double-digit numbers together until a single-digit soul number between 1 and 9 is reached. If a Soul Number is 11, 22, or 33, it will not decrease to 2, 4, or 6. It remains 11, 22, or 33 and becomes several souls 11/2, 22/4, or 33/6.

8+1+9 = 18

<u>1+8</u> = 9 Soul number

THE PERSONALITY NUMBER

The Personality Number of the seven Personality Numbers is the least important. It is also known as the Outer You or the Outer Personality Number because it gives an indication of how others perceive you and are said to represent the "outer you" in your birth certificate name.

HOW TO CALCULATE THE PERSONALITY NUMBER

Step 1: Add the consonant numbers in your birth certificate name.

Step 2: To create specific numbers, insert every title separately. To create a single number sum, add double-digit numbers together (unless they equal 11, 22, or 33, which remain 11, 22, or 33).

M A R YA N NS M I T H

4 + 9	5+5	1+4 + 2+8
13	10	15
1+3	1+0	1+5
4	1	6

Step 3: Add the single figures together (or 11, 22, and 33 if applicable) and continue to add any double-digit numbers together until you get a single-digit number between 1 and 9. If the total number of a character is 11, 22, or 33, it does not decrease to 2, 4, or 6. This stays 11, 22, and 33 and becomes a Personality number of 11/2, 22/4, and 33/6.

4+1+6 = 11/2 Personality Number

THE MATURITY NUMBER

The maturity figure in your table is a very significant number because it shows your future potential and your life's ultimate goal. It tells you where your destiny is taking you and what you can expect from the second half of your life. It is also known at the Power Number, Attainment Number, or Realization Number. In making long-term goals and choices, it is the amount to keep in mind.

HOW TO CALCULATE THE MATURITY NUMBER

The Maturity Number is calculated by adding the Life Path Number and Destiny Number together.

Step 1: Add the number of your life path and the destiny figure.

Step 2: To create a single-digit maturity figure, add any double-digit numbers together unless they equal 11, 22, and 33, and then become a maturity number of 11/2, 22/4, and 33/6.

For instance, let's use Mary Ann Smith's 3 Life Path Number and 11/2 Destiny Number;

3 Life Path Number + 11/2 Destiny Number = 14

<u>1+4</u> = 5 Maturity Number

THE CURRENT NAME NUMBER

The Current Name Number is the name you actually use on a daily basis, which is the "first" and "last." Often known as the Mini Expression Number, it is a shortened version of the title of the birth certificate for some individuals. For others, because of wedding, birth, or some other excuse, it is a completely new title.

The Current Name Number is an indicator of the pulse that you project into the universe whenever you use the name. It is your "energetic fingerprint," which incorporates the current number profile with new personality traits, talents, teachings, interactions, and opportunities.

HOW TO CALCULATE THE CURRENT NAME NUMBER

The Current Name Number of the title is determined using the same formula used to calculate the Destiny Number. Please note that one title is considered to be a hyphenated or hybrid name.

For instance, let's use Mary Ann Smith's current and married name, Mary Jones:

M A R YJ O N E S

4+1+9+71+6+5+5+1

21 18

2+1 = 3   1+8 = 9

3+9 = 12

1+2 = 3 Current Name Number

THE BIRTHDAY NUMBER

The Birth Day Number is just the "day" of the month on which you were born and is otherwise known as the Day Number or the Day Born Number. It reveals additional traits of personality along with specific talents and abilities that will assist you on your path of life.

HOW TO CALCULATE THE BIRTHDAY NUMBER

Reduce to a single-digit number the day of the month you were born.

If you were born on a single-digit day, that is the Birth Day Number, and if you were born on a double-digit day, apply the numbers to a single-digit Birth Day Number together.

If you were born on the 11th and 29th, it would become an 11/2 Birth Day Number, and the 22nd is a Birth Day Number of 22/4.

For instance:

June 8, 1972 = 8 Birth Day number

April 23, 1983 = 2+3 = 5 Birth Day number

December 29, 2001 = 2+9 = 11/2 Birth Day number

May 22, 1954 = 22/4 Birth Day number

Chapter 2: Basic Elements Of Numerology

A Numerology Chart has eleven components. Eight of them:

The Life Path (or Destiny Pattern) number,

The Expression Number,

The Ambition (or Heart's Desire) Number,

The Personality (or Impression) Number,

The Birthday Vibration

The Concord

The Planes of Expression, and

The Intensification Tables

relate to people - the nature of the self and its purpose in this life. They reveal traits and talents, strengths and weaknesses, good points and bad ones.

The remaining three:

The Pinnacles,

The Cycles, and

The Challenges deal with events and the timing of events, and reveal what the Life Path is likely to be like at a given point in time - paths to be followed, pitfalls to be avoided, obstacles to be surmounted, opportunities to be seized.

Which Numbers are Used?

Numerology allocates meaning only to the Primary Numbers 1 through 9, and to the Master Numbers 11 and 22. This means that in every case figure totals have to be reduced to a Primary or a Master Number, i.e. 31 would be reduced to 4 (3 + 1 = 4), and 92 would be reduced to 11 (9 + 2 = 11).

How Do Letters Become Numbers?

The alphabet is translated into Primary Numbers by way of this standard numbers-to-letters chart:

1	2	3	4	5	6	7	8	9
A	B	C	D	E	F	G	H	I

J	K	L	M	N	O	P	Q	R
S	T	U	V	W	X	Y	Z	

You will find a numbers-to-letters chart to help you find your personal numbers in each of the relevant Chapters.

Calculating Major 'Personal Numbers'

The five major 'personal numbers' of a numerology chart are calculated as follows:

1. The Life Path or Destiny Pattern Number is found by adding the day, month and year of birth, and reducing the answer to a single digit. For example, the Life Path number for 4th March 1960 would be 5, i.e.: 4 + 3 + 1 + 9 + 6 = 23. 2 + 3 = 5.

2. The Expression Number is found by translating the letters of the full name into numbers using the numbers-to-letters chart, then adding up the numbers, and reducing the answer to a single digit., e.g. JANE = 1+1+5+5 =12. 1+2 = 3.

3. The Ambition or Heart's Desire Number is found by translating the vowels of the full name into numbers, adding them up, and reducing the answer to a single digit, e.g. JANE = 1(A) + 5(E) = 6. Y is treated as a vowel when there is no vowel in the name. 'Lynn', for example, produces an Ambition Number 7.

4. The Personality Number is found by translating the consonants of the full name into numbers, adding them up, and reducing them to a single digit, e.g. JANE = 1(J) + 5(N) = 6.

5. The Birthday Vibration is the day of birth in any month of any year.

You do not have to remember how to make these calculations now; you will be reminded of the formula for each calculation when you arrive at the Chapter dealing with that particular aspect of your Chart.

Making Your Own Chart

Making a Chart for yourself is simple, but because it involves using a letters-to-numbers chart, making calculations, and then using those figures to make fresh calculations, it is definitely a 'hard copy' project. You will need a notebook and pencil and – because accidents happen and anyone can make a mistake – an eraser and a calculator.

It is best to work slowly, and check all of your figures very carefully at least twice to make sure that you have not made any mistakes. One wrong number somewhere can make a nonsense of a big chunk of your Chart.

Working with Keywords and Meanings

Each Primary or Master Number has a specific set of meanings. Sometimes those meanings differ slightly within specific categories – when a particular number relates to the Expression, for example, rather than to the Life Path – but the differences are very marginal, and occur only because one or another aspect of a number can be rendered more important by virtue of its appearance within a particular category.

Keywords are mnemonics, i.e.: they reduce the many attributes of each number to a few bare, readily memorable essentials. However, whilst it is possible to go a long way toward constructing and understanding a Chart using Keywords only, the meaning of a particular number and the effect it produces when it predominates in a Chart, or appears as any one of the major 'personal numbers' in a Chart, is obviously very important and all of the information (however lengthy!) relating to that number therefore needs to be read and considered very carefully.

The Advantages of Using a Ghost

Because most people find it difficult to be objective about their own numbers, it is a good idea to start your career in numerology by making a note of all your own numbers, then setting them aside for a while and interpreting numbers that belong to someone else – preferably NOT someone you know. We shall be working with a 'ghost' throughout this book. This will allow you to learn about numbers and practice calculating and interpreting them for someone suitably anonymous before you start working with your own numbers and those of your relatives and friends.

Our ghost's name is Mary Jane Smith. Mary Jane is purely a figment of my imagination. I decided upon Mary Jane's name and chose 29th September 1963 as her date of birth. So far as her Chart is concerned, the present year is 1990 and Mary Jane is 27 years old. Any resemblance between our ghost and anyone living or dead is therefore purely accidental. Think of her as your first client!

Making Notes

Final interpretation of any Numerology Chart is much easier if you take the time to make comprehensive notes – i.e. notes that are not solely constructed of or reliant upon Keywords - as you go along.

I have made 'Ghost Notes' that relate to Mary Jane Smith's Chart in each Chapter – but they take the form of a series of questions, and are relatively short and far from comprehensive. If you choose to work with Mary Jane, you will therefore need to consider those questions, think your own thoughts, ask your own questions, and draw your own conclusions just as you would have to if you were working on your own Chart or that of a relative or friend.

Best Practice

When you make notes relating to any Chart, best practice is to always begin by stating the obvious, e.g.:

Name: Mary Jane Smith

Date of Birth: 29th September 1963

Present Age: 27

Present Year: 1990

You will be making several separate sets of notes relating to many different categories. Always remind yourself of which particular category you are working with at any given time and what that category is about, and always supply yourself with a full set of calculations e.g.:

Category: Life Path

Calculation: Day 29

(2 + 9 = 11 = 1 + 1 = 2)

Month 9 = 9

Year 1963

(1 + 9 + 6 + 3 = 19 = 10 = 1 + 0 = 1)

2 + 9 + 1 = 12, 1 + 2 = Life Path 3

Always begin by making brief notes about the Life Path Number, even though you may feel that you have little useful to say at that point. The Life Path Number is a skeleton that other numbers will cloth in flesh – and that process becomes much easier if you have the 'bones' down in black and white.

This method of making notes might appear to be time-consuming and unnecessary. You should bear in mind, though, that there may well come a day when you are working on more than one Chart at once. It is really important to be able to readily identify the person to whom your notes and calculations belong.

Interpreting Your Results

Honesty has always been the best policy in every area of life, but honesty is particularly important when it comes to interpreting the numbers that make up a Numerology Chart.

Numbers don't lie, but human beings often tend to lie to themselves about unpalatable personal truths.

It is important to be aware that numbers have negative as well as positive qualities, and that numbers that are poorly represented in a Chart (or absent from it altogether) are just as important as those that are present. There is no point in pretending that negatives are not there, or that the good stuff is better than it really is.

Is Interpretation a 'Psychic Art'?

I am not sure whether interpretation is or is not a 'psychic art' - but it is certainly something best undertaken by a human being. There is a lot of numerology software around – and it is very nice to have all those calculations completed accurately and quickly and effortlessly – but whilst the software is clever, labour saving, and capable of stating the obvious, it cannot make intuitive connections between one set of calculations and another. As a result, its interpretations are mechanical, lifeless and 'flat', and factors that would be picked up instantly by a human being are often not touched upon at all.

I believe – as did the psychologist Jung – that numbers are potent symbols that speak directly to the unconscious mind. I therefore have no doubt that your unconscious mind will provide you with many insights as you work your way through the different sections that will together make up any Chart you decide to work on, whether you think of yourself as being 'psychic' or not.

Chapter 3: The History Of Numerology

Numerology, in one guise or another has been utilized throughout the history of the human race. Numerology is the relationship between numbers and events and the interpretation as to how they can impact life. It is possible to use numerology to learn more about yourself and to discover hidden talents, but it is so versatile in that it can be used to ascertain information about health, finances, career opportunities or even relationships. Although the term numerology did not manifest until the 1900's, the concept has been around throughout the centuries and if you use it regularly, it becomes an easy addition to life.

To understand numerology, we must turn our minds back to a time when the Greeks were using pebbles so to understand geometry and arithmetic. As such, a numeric value was assigned to each of the letters and to be able to determine the key values of any word, letter values were added together so to form a single number.

This is a practice known as isopsephy and those who use this system believed that there is a divine connection between any words and phrases which share equal numerical values. At the time, it was used to predict future trends within battles. This technique was used in both Hebrew and Arabic alphabets. Due to varying beliefs and cultures, there have been various forms of numerology.

Chaldean numerology

Often known as Mystic numerology, Chaldean numerology is older than Pythagorean – which is the system we use within this course. Chaldean numerology is less popular simply because it is complex and therefore, is more difficult to calculate. It is based on sounds of vibrations and to simplify, the numbers are assigned to vibrations - those best believed to suit rather than being used in sequential order. Each number has an energy, and these were considered relative to certain planets and heavenly bodies. It is said that those who practice this form of Chaldean numerology also believe that it carries both spiritual and mystical messages.

Pythagorean numerology is different in how it calculates results. Letters are assigned numbers 1-9 based on where they fall in the alphabet.
Chinese numerology

Chinese numerology is different from others as it considers some numbers to be very lucky while others are extremely unlucky. Certainly, throughout Eastern culture, luck plays a significant role and is often interlinked with fate. In Chinese numerology, it can be deemed that someone who is unlucky is simply following their destiny. In this type of numerology, the meanings are formed by how the number sounds when spoken out loud. If it sounds like a word, then this would be unlucky, and the number would also be considered the same.

Pythagorean numerology

Pythagorean numerology is the most popular form and the easiest when it comes to learning the principles although it can still seem to be complex. The trick to learning it and using it properly is to study and try one or two techniques at a time. Numbers are used to quantify and record everything but are not deemed as having mystical qualities. Each object has a unique vibration and the higher the vibration, the greater the positive energy.

The lower the vibration, the lower the energy levels or, it can represent negative energy.

In Pythagorean numerology, numbers measure that energy so numbers 1 through to 9 symbolizes the nine stages of human life. The science of numbers continues to evolve, and it also forms spiritual foundations for many societies such as the Masons or even Theosophical societies.

In Pythagorean numerology, it is possible to analyze someone's full birth name as well as their date of birth. Therefore, a given name provides a unique insight into that person and will determine their natural skills and talents, personality traits, motivations and inner desires. When the birthdate is analyzed, it can reveal distinctive life patterns and this includes health and wellbeing, love or whether financial success is possible. It can also indicate timing - when to finish a relationship or when to make a career change.

Numerology today.

If you have not used numerology before, it's good to know that the possibilities are endless. The more you use it, the greater the opportunities to do so. Above all else, it is fun. Use it to discover if it is the right time to meet someone new or, if in an existing relationship, whether it is time to call it a day. It can be used to decide the best date for marriage or to start a new business or, for changing your name or to find a good holiday destination. Numerology can be used in every facet of life once you understand the basics.

Chapter 4: The Astrological Idea

Rational Western thought for the last 300 years, since Descartes and the Cogito, finds it difficult to grasp the astrological signs as complex structures aspiring toward unity.

In essence, the nature of each sign as an idiom – the idea of an archetype in the soul of man – creates a form of generalization and flow to a synthetic principle from one surrounded by a particular core. Understanding this idea clearly is like opening a window to a fascinating world of characters and astrological situations, 12 in number.

When the sun is in Aquarius, from January 21 to February 19, the "macro" influence is indeed Aquarian. Each individual sign, however, absorbs thought, energy, or an archetypal situation in a particular area of its solar chart, which begins with that sign in the opening position, the First House, followed by the others in their respective order. When the sun is in Aquarius, for all Taurus this is the 10th house: the house of careers, work, authority, adult figures, crucial decisions, contractions, and time pressure. In each instance, Taurus will undergo, in one way or another, something in relation to the above 10th house motifs. There will be individual differences in the nature of the events; however, the thought, the pattern, the idiom, will be the same: shrinkage or contraction, boundaries and time pressures. For Pisces, in this solar position, there will be a decline in energy for all the Pisces in the world — yes, exactly what you read — in spite of the fact that you are a unique Pisces. At any rate, you are with the Pisces in Tokyo, London, New York, or wherever — all of you will be in the position of 12th house, an archetypal pattern associated with feelings of self-sacrifice, concession, victimization, inertia, confusion, and even institutionalization.

A decline in energy level does not work according to a scientific, logical plan. This is a description of a situation with many possibilities: The Pisces in Tokyo may experience a business loss, the Pisces in London may be hospitalized, the Pisces in New York may feel an unwillingness to communicate and will isolate himself. They all react according to the pattern but in a different way. Inertia and a decline in energy level characterize all. This is the philosophy of generalization, which opposes rational Western thought. Generalization evolves from the idea of divine unity, which expresses itself and influences us through twelve superior forms: twelve archetypes and the scaffold — the mathematical-geometric skeleton — is the celestial Zodiac. The "journey of the sun" along the 360 degrees of the Tropic of Cancer, 30 degrees for each sign or house, is without a doubt an abstract philosophic idea which is difficult to accept although possible to experience and to follow. When the sun is in Taurus, a general planetary influence might be felt in the area of economics; however, not for Aries, who experiences aspirations toward the null and void in a mystical sense and a type of entropy, at the same time that Capricorn and Virgo have dynamic surges of energy and activity. The vital and extroverted 5th and 9th houses are activated when the sun is in Taurus, while Aries finds itself in Taurus' 12th house.

This is a relative and complex structure, since divinity as a unifying principle draws us inward through archetypes and generalizations. According to the principle of reductionism, which represents a maximum of attributes in a minimal common denominator, I will try to explain this as it pertains to astrology.

The celestial picture changes every four minutes in accordance with the movement of the earth. Twins born within this four-minute time span will experience identical planetary influences throughout life. Let us suppose for the moment that the planet Uranus forms a sharp angle to the planet Venus in the twins' natal chart. It is a powerful astrological fact that Uranus causes distance and disruption. At age 28, one twin gets divorced due to his wife's decision to leave him forever – finished! His twin brother's wife, at the same time, is hired for a job that takes her abroad several times a month. The divine-idiom-archetype here is the disruption, the separation, the distance; and both twins experienced this. The results of this were different, as they depended upon the free choice of the individual. The mold is the same, but the end result creates a differing story. The first gets divorced; the second experiences detachment based on objective rather than emotional circumstances, as far as this leads one to believe, of course. (As it was, the wife applied for the job abroad in order to "take a breather from that nudnik.....")

Astrology is concerned with the understanding of these molds or patterns. Each individual event may be interpreted differently, as the principle of freechoice which exists in each of us operates within existing and expected options.

One can view the archetypal framework also in the story of Yael, Aquarius, who came to me for astrological advice and counseling. Yael was an Air Force officer and following discharge, began to work for a computer company. She decided to change jobs and switched to one in communications production. Changes? Only superficially. Communications is connected to Aquarius, as is the Air Force and aircraft. Yael could also work at NASA or with dolphins, as these are also Aquarian in nature. The principle is the same: the Aquarian idea.

Every individual has a personal astrological chart, however he is also a part of the idiom of his sign in the sense of divine law, a superior archetypal model, which forms all of our spiritual reality as individuals and as a species. Astrology shows us what the Divine thinks of us, and there is a program, a plan, and a regulatory order that will enable us, by means of this book, to sample, to understand, and to apply it.

The truth is that one can calculate a unique and personal natal chart, but it does not liberate the individual from the never-ending dialog between him and the Supreme Sovereign – the "boss on-high". From the time that we are born, and we are born the minute that the universe dials our number, the soul enters the energy field – according to geometric and mathematical patterns – in a form known as "sign X". From here, in an exact order, the accompanying, all-inclusive system is formed: the remaining signs, which we cannot change, as we have already been born. We already know the game, although not completely. It is possible to understand and to act upon it with additional wisdom. Fact: when the sun is in Sagittarius, it is in the 8th house of Taurus. There exists danger from cheaters, loss, and breakdowns, corruption, and forgery. The knowledge of this will enable the individual to minimize the potential damage and to take extra care in attempts to prevent it.

Astrology is a closed mathematical structure; however, within this structure, individuals have the freedom of choice. One must only be aware of the rules of the game. When known, they can be of great benefit to us and for us. In addition, the individual is the director, the producer, and the actor of his own life. The scenic background, the costumes, and the stage are provided. What he must do now is write the script. The raw materials are the energies of the planets and the twelve signs of the Zodiac. The timing and meaning of events are areas so broad in range and scope as to enable the actor to create the script in many different versions, provided that he is familiar with the tools and the subject matter. The story would be much like as seen in the movie "Sliding Doors."

It must be understood that astrology is not an exact science, as it is defined today. Rather, astrology is a language, an art, a philosophy, and an experience, and therefore, is open to many interpretations.

Neptune is the planet of illusions, self-destruction, and complications; however, it is also the height of creativity and personal achievement. The interpretation is subjective and open to choice. The individual is the architect and builder of his life; the bricks, stone, and mortar are divine gifts from the superior force of energy from which we are inspired.

We have at hand twelve tools or entities, which, in essence, are the twelve knights of King Arthur's round table, the Twelve Tribes of Israel, the twelve apostles, and the twelve students of Buddha. Fact or coincidence? Now it is our turn to make something good of this, and therefore, it is essential to understand them. The energy and the archetypes, open of substance, do not conform to statistical measurement or a game of darts. Astrology is not found on a target range but in life. As we know, in life, there are many more situations and possibilities than there exist in a dart game. The astrologer is asked to be authentic and to choose between astrology as a science – through determinism, closure, and life as a pre-determined fate with no thought or creativity - and the idea of archetypes and life as a playing field of communication between the soul and the Creator. With archetypes, instead of science we have a spacing of events within optional boundaries and the possibility of wide creative improvement and perfection in a nondeterministic manner.

I attempted to define the limits of possibility in representation of astrological and numerological situations, mainly in order to teach a type of understanding and contemplation of the flow of time and events in our lives.

As you will read, in each situation I presented several possibilities in order that the system would remain open for interpretation of the reader. It is understood that there is the precise data of one's personal natal chart, which I am not able to view, of course. Gray areas, ambivalence, and paradoxes are the substance of astrology, and the idea of either-or would be incorrect in this instance. Instead we have this but also that.

Occasionally there are uncertain and blurred situations, as in the grain of sand in the eye of Castenada's Don Juan. When one tries to see it, it escapes, but in a time of bewilderment or contemplation, it suddenly appears in full view. Let yourself be perplexed and in the corner of your eye you will notice mind-boggling things. From a direct viewpoint, that of Descartes, they are hidden – do not allow this view to conquer your soul, which is much stronger and more liberated.

Chapter 5: A Misunderstood Art Form

The study and implementation of basic numerology is one of the easiest occult arts that can be learned; however, it seems that it is the least understood. The fact that numbers represent unseen forces, with direct ties to the occult, has made numerology nearly taboo in western society. However, if you practice numerology correctly, then you should be able to gain and clearer understanding of the direction in which your life is going. What's more is that numerology can actually provide you with insight into things you need to do to achieve improvements in the areas of your life that need it the most.

It is thought that numerology is useful for every aspect of life, from understanding changes in your life and gaining insight into psychologically difficult situations surrounding you to enhancing your intuition. In addition, those who closely study and follow numerology say that they can even use the information they gain from their research to perform tasks like choosing names for their children or even what type of house to purchase.

Even one of the developers of the numerological system, Pythagoras, did not fully understand the power behind the numbers with which he toiled. At the time, the basic appreciation of numerology came not from its mystical qualities, but more so from the fact that numbers tend to be more practical than physical objects, not to mention numbers were more precise. Pythagoras, and other philosophers, scientists, and mathematicians all believed at the time that everything in the material world had mathematical relationships to one another and the whole realm surrounding them.

It was assumed that finding out about said relationships between numbers and the physical plane was a task for your mind and spirit to explore, only being revealed by divine grace once you had completed several levels of study. St. Augustine (of Hippo) was recorded to have said about numerology, "Numbers are the Universal language offered by the deity to humans as confirmation of the truth." This quote was uttered during St. Augustine's lifetime (A.D. 354 – 430), and it just as true today as it was then.

Chapter 6: Basic Understanding Toward Numerology?

Numerology is the analysis of numbers, specifically one's date of birth, and the associated numerical values given to the letters of the alphabet, specifically one's name. Numerology also examines such numbers and their extraordinary effects on one's life and associated energy vibrations, along with the interpretation of such information to provide insight and guidance.

Numerology is a science that allows practitioners to help their clients learn more about who they are, what they can become, and what they can expect in the years ahead. However, it also brings some practitioners far beyond that; to a place where knowledge stops being theory and becomes an experience. I hope you will become such a practitioner.

As per oxford dictionary Numerology is the branch of knowledge that deals with occult significance of numbers. In numerology Astrologer relates each numbers and alphabetical characters to particular number and believes that the particular number has some sort of cosmic vibration. As per Hindu astrology, Astrologer builds relation between numbers and alphabetical characters to a particular Number from 1 to 9 and each number from 1 to 9 is represented by Planets. For example: Number 1 represented by Planet Sun, Number 2 represented by Planet Moon etc. These planets (1-9 numbers) are influencing individual's characteristics.

No one exactly knows the origin of Numerology and when it started. The Pythagorean and Chaldean schools of numbers are the most commonly used. Pythagorean system is more popular especially in West but Chaldean Numerology is older. In this website,

Chaldean Numerology has been used to determine Alphabetical numbers.

Pythagoras was a master mathematician born in Greece in the 6th century B.C; we all are familiar with his geometry theorems. However, He is also considered as a Farther of Modern Numerology. He spent many years of study in Egypt and other parts of the world and explore the ancient science of numbers. After that he brought his knowledge and experience to Greece and taught nearly forty years and established a college and philosophy of numbers.

There was a time when Astrology, Numerology and other occult studies were considered a religion not in the way we would know it today. Around 356 B.C; In the time of Alexander the Great, the Chaldeans believed that their knowledge of Numerology and Astrology went back at least 473,000 years. The Chaldean system of numbers is still in use today. The

Chaldean system of numbers are also known as Mystic Numerology.

What are the number's in Numerology?

Single digit Number: Number from 1 to 9 are called single digit number and each number signifies particular properties.

Two-digit Number:

Master number: Number 11, 22 and 33 are Master Number, these numbers are very spiritual in nature and it has its unique characteristics.

Karmic Debt Number: Number 13, 14, 16 and 19 are Karmic Debt Number.

CORE NUMBERS: In numerology there are 5 main number which are considered as a CORE NUMBER, it is like building blocks for you. The two numbers come from your date of birth and three numbers comes from your Name number. The two numbers which comes from your date of birth are

Life path number

Birth day number

The remaining three numbers are calculated based on your Name. the three numbers come from your name are

Expression Number

Personality Number

Heart's desire Number

1. Life Path Number: One of the most important numbers from the perspective of Numerology is Life Path number. With the help of Life Path Number, one can understand their personalities, Challenges and Opportunities one will encounter during this lifetime. Since this is related to your date of birth, this number helps you to identify momentum and direction of your life.

2. Birthday Number: This is another number which deals with your personality and ability to deals with particular area. Life Path Number definitely influences your personality but I have seen Birthday number is influencing your personality

more at conscious level. The Birthday number gets calculated on the day you born. This is one of the number among Core Number. Birthday number possess some special talent you have. It is a gift to you that will help you along your life's path.

3. Expression Number: The Expression number helps individual to know about their strength and weaknesses. The Life Path number tells you life's lesson and how you handle them while Expression number tells you about your area of natural strength and weaknesses. This number is very important and it should be compatible with your Life Path number. If your life path number tells you goal, this number tells you the ability to achieve that.

4. Personality Number: The personality number is the first impression you make on other people. This number telling about the area of yourself which you are usually ready and willing to revel to the world.

This number also helps you to determine how much you should reveal and to whom. This number acts as a buffer, screening out some people and situations you don't want to deal with while welcoming the things in life that relate to your inner nature.

5. Heart Desire Number: The Heart desire number is what you really want in your life and in your love life as well. This number tells you the reason behind the choice you make in all aspects of your life it is either your career or your relationship this is all about your burning fire within.

Chapter 7: How To Outline Your Numerology Life Profile

The numerology profile of a person is composed of several and different numbers. Each one is going to represent a specific thing in your life. The type of numbers you get will vary dependingon where you get your readings. Some sources will be able to provide you with an extensive list while others will just give you the basics.

Numerology is the study of how numbers affect our lives. Every person is going to have a set of numbers in the profile. These are reduced from the birth date, the birth name, or both. Some ofthe most prominent numbers in our profiles are the Life Path Number, the Destiny Number, and the Personality Number. The names for these numbers may vary from one numerology resource to another.

BIRTHDAY

The day you were born bears great significance in understanding who you are and where your talents lie. The day of birth indicates some special talent you possess. It is a gift to you that will help you along your Life's Path. Your day of birth is one of your five Core numbers, the Life Path, Expression, Heart's Desire, and Personality being the other four. It is the least significant of the five numbers, but perhaps the most finite, in that it reveals a specific ability you possess in a marked degree.

Your Birthday is 17

You are highly ambitious and blessed with excellent business and financial instincts. Your approach to business is original, creative, and daring. You are highly independent. You have very sound judgment. You are an excellent manager and organizer. You are gifted with the ability to see the larger picture, and, remarkably, how the details come into play. You are efficient and can handle large projects. Your challenge is to avoid becoming obsessed with your own judgment and power to the point that you refuse to delegate authority or responsibility to others. You can easily slip into the role of dictator, benevolent or otherwise, feeling that you and only you have the sufficiently sound judgment to guide the ship. You are self-confident and have high expectations for yourself. Interestingly, the expectations of others stimulate you, especially if they doubt you can pull off what you intend to do. you tend to be dramatic, especially with money. You have a need for status and may show off the fruits of your labour with an impressive car or house.

Whether it is business or socially oriented, you have a big dream. Your ambitions spread out far and wide and you will not rest until you have placed your mark on the world. You love your home and family and like to be complimented. Avoid becoming domineering or possessive of your enterprise. Share the fruits of your labours with others, which will multiply your pleasure manifold.

When decoding your own name, it's important to realize that in Numerology, each letter in your name has a corresponding number and that the placement of each letter determines the kind of influence that letter (and its numerological meaning) has on you. To simplify things, we will referto letters and their numerological meaning rather than discuss the precise numbers they translate into.

The Cornerstone

First, let's look at the Cornerstone. This is the first letter of your name. It provides general insight about your essential personality, and it has a lot to say about your approach to life's speed bumps and open doors. In other words: your Cornerstone is all about how you approach both difficulties and upswings.

The Capstone

The Capstone is the last letter of your name, and, fittingly, it demonstrates your ability to see projects and ideas through to the end. This translates into your "finishing" number. When you look at your Cornerstone and Capstone -- the letters that "bookend" your name you can determine how easy it is for you to start and stop important processes and projects.

First letter

According to numerology, the letters of your baby's name can help you understand more about her potential, and how she'll achieve personal fulfilment. It can also tell you what obstacles or opportunities she'll face in her future.

Numerology links each letter of the alphabet with a number between 1 and 9. Each number has a specific set of traits and qualities associated with it.

All the letters of your baby's name will have some kind of meaning. But the first letter of her first name will be the most powerful, with the most intrinsic energy.

If you're trying to choose a baby name, find out in our guide below what the first letter could spell out for your baby's future.

Letter A:

The first letter, associated with the first number, A is a powerful initial to give your baby. It acts as a strong indicator of her future leadership ability and will help her with planning and innovation.

People with the initial A project self-confidence, ambition, initiative, originality, strength and willpower. This letter can, therefore, bring your baby great energy and creativity.

Letter B:

This letter has an aura of serenity and contentment. With the initial B, your baby will have a spiritual leaning, which may bring him great happiness in life.

As your baby grows, he's likely to be family-oriented, with a generous soul and a warm heart. He'll love nature and animals too.

This emotional streak cuts both ways though, as some people influenced by B can take things too personally.

Letter C:

Those motivated by the letter C are impulsive and joyful people. Giving your baby this initial, means she'll thrive on movement and change, and always seek out and appreciate new experiences.

Driven by intuition, people with the initial C can take on too much at once, and may not alwaysfinish what they start.

Letter D:

The letter D signifies balance and harmony. Your baby will be practical, self-disciplined and persistent in striving for his goals if influenced by this initiative.

Your baby may make a great leader with the initial D. He'll cope well with responsibility, and will enjoy taking on grand challenges.

Letter E:

The letter E conveys joyfulness, generosity and a great sense of humour. If you give your baby this initial, she'll be chatty and free-spirited. She's also likely to be highly active, and enjoy thefiner things in life.

Letter F:

If your baby's name begins with the letter F, he'll have a strong desire to help others. Tender and loving with a calm temperament, people with this initial make great peacekeepers who can resolve any conflict.

Letter G:

The letter G conveys great stability. If your baby's influenced by it, she'll be self-sufficient and will look inwards to learn more about herself. This will allow her to make the best of her natural talents.

People with the initial G are satisfied with doing good work for its own sake, rather than demanding great rewards. However, this independence also means that they're sometimes stubborn and impatient with others.

Letter H:

People associated with the letter H are always on the go. With a strong inner drive, your babywill gain great self-control, stamina and endurance from this initiative. This will help him to achieve his goals.

In addition, H often brings creative skills. So you may want to encourage your baby's artistic pursuits if you choose this letter.

Letter I:

A name beginning with I will inspire your baby to be humane, generous and enthusiastic. She'll often put others' needs before her own, meaning she'll make a good counsellor, psychologist or teacher.

Letter J:

Above all, the letter J is associated with kindness. If your baby's name starts with J, he's sure to be family-oriented, and he may seek a career that fits around his personal commitments.

This initiative also brings creativity, intelligence and exuberance, which will help your baby to succeed.

Letter K:

This letter projects energy, originality, authority and leadership qualities. Your baby is sure to have great spiritual and physical energy with this initial, which she'll use to help others.

Letter L:

This letter radiates wisdom, dedication and imagination. Your baby is destined to complete everything he sets out to do and to help those less fortunate than him.

Letter M:

M is a happy, optimistic letter with great creative vibrations. It will influence your baby to be cheerful and to have a great love of home and hearth.

As your baby grows, the letter M means she'll be proud to stand up for those she loves. She'll also act as a strong advocate for the causes she supports.

Letter N:

The letter N is associated with intelligence and imagination, as well as the determination to put plans into practice.

Giving your baby this initial means he'll grow up to take great pride in overcoming obstacles and will successfully find his own path in life. This may make him intriguing to others!

Letter O:

The letter O has strong spiritual vibrations, which can bring great insight. Giving your baby this initial will power her by an inner light. She'll grow up fair, just and brave.

Your baby is also sure to make an excellent mediator, and have the skills to easily achieve her professional aims.

Letter P:

The letter P will bring your baby a fascinating combination of common sense, order and reason, and a hearty dose of creative talent too. He'll love to learn all he can, and will happily expresswhat he's learned to others.

Your baby will enjoy success and will like to surround himself with gifted or influential individuals who can help him understand the world.

Letter Q:

This is a letter that projects confidence, persistence and calm. If you give your baby the initial Q, she'll probably grow to be intense and quick-witted, with great intuition.

With Q leading your baby, she's destined to become a leader rather than a follower. She'll often take an interest in the unusual side of life and will occupy her mind with the strange and cryptic.

Letter R:

The letter R represents a soft, kind and gentle spirit. If your baby has this initial, he'll have a positive, idealistic outlook on life, and will love helping others.

Your baby may well become a bohemian eccentric who loves all people and goes to great lengthsto help them. His honest and trusting nature will often win him respect from those around him.

Letter S:

The letter S is associated with a strong and dedicated spirit. Giving your baby this initial will project an ability to weather any hardship and make it through difficult times. She'll also have the power to realize her dreams and build her ideal future.

Letter T:

This letter conveys great patience, tolerance and kindness. Those touched by the letter T have excellent leadership qualities and may be seen as a dominant force in their workplaces or friendship groups.

Giving your baby this initial will mean he's likely to share his knowledge and possessions freely with those he leads.

Letter U:

The letter U will bring a magical, mystical quality to your baby. She'll probably be talented and lucky, but she'll often find herself torn between duty and desire too.

Letter V:

If you choose V as your baby's first initial, he'll be creative, hard-working and loyal. Passionate and enthusiastic, those influenced by this letter often grow restless if they don't have the opportunity to move and explore.

Letter W:

This letter projects great willpower, strength and enthusiasm. If your baby bears this initial, she'll often be seen as charming and kind. This will help her get along with a wide variety of people.

Letter X:

Those rare souls with the initial X are constantly striving to better themselves, seeking perfection and balance in all things.

With the letter X, your baby will have a lively nature and show exceptional bravery. He'll also be happy to embrace change in his search for harmony.

Letter Y:

This initial brings great determination and both physical and spiritual energy to its bearer. If your baby's influenced by Y, she'll be highly analytical and intelligent, with the ability to quickly find solutions to her problems.

Letter Z:

The letter Z brings determination, persistence and fearlessness. With this initial, your baby will always finish what he starts, and he'll be highly organized and methodical.

Intuitive and fair-minded, your baby will make an excellent leader. However, some with this initiative can let their ambition run away with them, often at the cost of their personal relationships.

First Vowel

Now look to the first vowel of your first name, this letter gets to your core. Think of the deepest goals, urges and dreams that drive you in all you do, this is the letter offers a glimpse into this area of life. But this is a secretive letter because few people wear what it really is they want on their sleeve. This first vowel in your name indicates something that only your closest friends and trusted family members might know about you and it's also a very telling "window" to your soul!

You might know someone who for whatever reason changed the first vowel in their name. Although this is rare, it indicates a person who is uncomfortable with who they really are, at their core.

Chapter 8: Meaning Of Each Number

Pythagoras believed that numbers had souls. This means that every number is alive. It is also believed that numbers have magical properties distinct from each other. As such, every number has its own unique powers and carries a set of traits and qualities. Find out the meaning of each number.

Number 1

The number 1 is the first number, also called as the primordial force. Its essence lies in new beginnings and creation. It is characterized by positivity, relentless will, and pure energy.

This number is marked with powerful traits, such as strong leadership, confidence, and strength. It is also often referred to as the divine number for the One God. The Pythagoreans call it as the monad, which symbolizes the Creator.

The number 1 also signifies that it is time to take action in order to reap rewards. In the Tarot, 1 is the card of the Magician. This number symbolizes the beginning, the first cause or mover, and the first step to anything and everything. It is an auspicious number.

Number 2

The number 2 calls for duality and balance. It also signifies judgment, where two contrasting views or things are weighed. It also refers to equality. In the Far East, the number 2 is considered a lucky number. However, in the Pythagorean system, this number is very unlucky.

This number also refers to extremes. It can also be a sign of indecisiveness where you need to make a difficult choice. Although referred to as the number of balance, it is also considered a number of division. Some refer to it as the number of existence since nothing in the universe can ever exist without the two polarities (positive and negative). In the Tarot, 2 is the card of the High Priestess.

Number 3

The number 3 is closely associated with magic, intuition, and advantage. It also signifies creativity. Many people also believe that 3 refers to time: past, present, and future, or a beginning, middle, and end. The number 3 is considered a lucky number that usually signifies success and good fortune. As a number of magic, there are many rituals and spiritual practices that require something to be done three times in succession. In the Tarot, 3 is the Empress.

Number 4

No wonder tables, chairs, and even big structures, stand on four legs, or foundations. The number 4 signifies stability and a strong foundation. According to the Pythagorean system, the number 4 is a perfect number. It is also referred to as the number of the Earth and the elements (fire, air, water, and earth). In the Tarot, 4 is the Emperor card.

Number 5

The number 5 is a dynamic force, characterized by adventure and daring. It is also said to refer to the marriage between heaven and earth. In the tarot, the number 5 is the Hierophant, which also symbolizes harmony and peace. This number also urges that some action or adventure must be taken.

Number 6

The number 6 symbolizes love, beauty, and sex. According to the Pythagorean system, this number is the first perfect number. It also symbolizes luck. In the Christian Bible, it is written that God created the world in 6 days; therefore, 6 has been associated with creation and completion. In the tarot, 6 is the card of the Lover.

Number 7

The number 7 is esoteric and mystical. It also deals with the imagination and the occult. It is considered a very magical number and is also referred to as the number of perfection. In the Pythagorean system, the number 7 is called as the septad. In the Christian Bible, after God created the world in 6 days, God rested on the seventh day. As such, people have referred to 7 as a number of rest and also of completion. Some also refer to 7 as the number of the universe. In the Tarot, 7 is the Chariot card.

Number 8

Commonly known as the number of infinity, the number 8 represents success, abundance, and wealth. Since there is no end to this number, it also signifies momentum. It also symbolizes balance and harmony. In China, 8 is a number of prosperity. In the Tarot, 8 is the card of Justice and Strength.

Number 9

The number 9 is a sacred number. It is commonly referred to as the number of magic and harmony. In the Pythagorean system, 9 is considered unlucky and is called as the ennead. The number 9 is also believed to be the number of heaven. In the Tarot, 9 is the Hermit card, which symbolizes reflection and self-realization. There is a striking harmony that can be noticed with this number. When you multiply any number to 9 and add up all the digits, you will also end up with a 9. For example: 9 x 30 = 270 = 2 + 7 + 0 = 9.

Number 10

Generally, 10 should be considered a 1, as 1 + 0 = 1. However, 10 of itself has its own significant meaning. The number 10 is known as the number of completion. The Pythagoreans believe that 10 is the holiest number among all the numbers. 10 represents the completion of a cycle. In the Tarot, 10 is the Wheel of Fortune card. It must be noted that 10 being a holy number is relative. Therefore, it does not always mean a completion of a beautiful cycle. Like in Hinduism, just as there is a god of creation, there is also a god of destruction, which is considered as important in the role of creation, knowing that before something can be rebuilt, one must first be destroyed. Both are considered holy for being in accordance with the Divine will.

Chapter 9: Jupiter (Number – 3)

People who are born under the days 3, 12, 21 or 30 or the date total by adding all the digits of the date to single number which becomes 3 or as per numerology if the name total gives sum with the number 3 (like 3,12,21,30,39,48,57 etc) are coming under Jupiter power.

Number 3 indicates Jupiter and it gives energy to the entire world. These people are hardworking and sincere to their superiors. Humbleness, tolerance and respect to elders are the natural qualities of these people .They do things in a fair way and they follow their ancestor's path. They like to help others but do not take any help. These people with social responsibility do social work without any profit.

They fight fearlessly whoever their enemies are. After attaining adulthood, though they have freedom family responsibilities and affection stops them from leading a selfless life.

At last these people will work hard and earn a good name but they won't have fame or have a big position in their life. They will always have helping tendency and they will do any sacrifice for their family. These people fight for the dignity of the family, honour of the country and they do not indulge in any work that affects their dignity.

If the influence of the Jupiter reduces these people become lazy, wrest, pompous and likes gambling. They also behave badly and they don't have mercy. These qualities indicate the reduction in the power of Jupiter.

These people are affected by skin diseases. Even small diseases like rashes do not cure easily. It is better to prevent the disease Eczema which is not curable by treatments. So these people should be careful in the above mentioned issues.

People born under 3: They have good thoughts and they will lead a dignified and quality life. They gain fame in their mid-age. They must increase their physical and spiritual strength and they have to vent out their feelings in a calm way.

People born under 12: Their life becomes a penance in serving the people and they have inborn qualities of a man leading a sacrificial life. These people gain fame from selfless work and sacrifice but they must indulge in social works. They come to bear sorrows and responsibilities in young age itself.

People born under 21: They will become news reporters and they are people who can bring a change in the society. They are selfish, they expect recognition for sacrifice and they are taskmasters. Life gets better as their general knowledge and experience increases. Their life will be very difficult.

People born under 30: These people are brilliant with high absorption power and they like to lead a courageous life. Failures don't affect them. Being well-versed in arts they like to be alone.

Names and number 3:

You will be ruled by JUPITER or the number 3 if you have the name total as 3 by adding up all the alphabets numbers making a single digit. (**AR JOHN** = 1+2+1+7+5+5 = 21=2+1=3) But, remember that the people born under **3** (Either the date or sum of date digits) only can have names under 3. Then only it will give good results. For others it may give trouble and lot of failures in life.

So, check the numbers and alphabets in the introduction chapter and find your name digits or sum accordingly. If not lucky, change letters or names to good numbers as said above.

Good and Bad Numbers Under 3 (for names by adding all the alphabets' digits)

3- Indicates hard work, brilliance and victory. They will lead a harmonious life with step by step improvement

12- People with this number give astonishing speech. They happily accept the difficulties of others as their own. They work for the sake for others.

21- People with this number are concerned with their happiness and profit. They work hard and reach the top in the life. They can tackle anything with their wit. First half of life will be difficult and the next half will be harmonious.

30- Have good thinking. They do things as they like. Achieve victory for self satisfaction even if it is non-profitable.

39- Hard-working people whose fame is taken away by others even after achieving an excellent position. Always work for others and less healthy and are easily affected by skin diseases.

48- Involvement in religious practices. In spite of opposition they achieve a lot in social welfare measures. Face lot of difficulties and they do things which are apart from their capabilities. Fate plays havoc.

57- This number gives victory at the beginning but retreats soon. The quick improvement faced in the life suddenly stops and it step by step deteriorates and then they lead the life of a normal man.

66- This number indicates astonishing power, mastery in arts, support of government and lovely life.

75- People with this number become famous suddenly, gain lot of friends quickly, become a famous personality unexpectedly. They may become a writer.

84- Initial life will be difficult. They will benefit from travelling. Unwanted enemity prevails, worries increases. They don't get expected result for their work. Little bit of interest increases in religious activities.

93- Achieve great things, have good general knowledge, desires will be fulfilled and they gain fame from writing epic plays. Gain profit in different jobs.

102- This number indicates victory in the initial part of the life, fatigue in the middle part of the life and confusion in the end of the life. It is not a very good number.

Lucky days: 3, 9, 12, 18,21,27,30 are good (Either day or sum of the digits in date). Days under 3 and 9 will also help. These dates are important days too.

Unlucky days: 6, 15, and 24. Avoid all the good start-ups or do not start anything in life in these days.

Work/Business: May become teacher, clerk in bank, secretary, dignified government jobs, work in charitable institutions or may serve in the army or jobs involving speaking skill. They may also become a scientist, research scholar or accountant.

Marriage/ Life Partner: people under 3 may choose 3, 9 or 2 as their life partners. But probably they will marry the people with the same number i.e. 3.

Lucky Colours: Orange, Rose, Yellow, Red and Blue.

Lucky Stone: Topaz (Yellow Sapphire) & Amethyst.

Personalities Under Number 3:

ALEXANDER GRAHAM BELL – 03-03-1847 - (3 & 8)

ABRAHAM LINCOLIN – 12-02-1809 – (3 & 5)

SWAMI VIVEKANANDA – 12-01-1863 – (3 & 4)

Chapter 10: Clear As Crystal; Crystal Healing Facts

If you are reading this book on an electronic device (e-book reader, computer, smart-phone) then you're already utilizing the power of crystals. Even if you're reading it in a more physical form the process by which a print copy has been produced will have involved some form of technology in which crystals played a part!

While using crystals within a technological setting may be a standard part of our lives – even if we are not aware of just how many of our existing technological advancements depend on them – some people find it a more difficult concept to understand that crystals can do more than store information or be used to transmit or create electricity.

In fact, crystal healing has long been practiced in many traditional settings – particularly in religious and healing traditions in India and the Far East. In the last century this practice has become more widely established in the west and is now accepted by many as an integral part of many healing traditions.

How Does Crystal Healing Work?

Energy is a force that resonates and radiates throughout everything in the universe. Without energy nothing could exist and our own bodies are vibrant with this essential life force. Ill-health is, in part, a manifestation of imbalances within the natural energy field that operates around us. Where these imbalances occur it is possible to use different kinds of energy to re-balance them. Hunger can be dissipated with the energy in our food and cancerous tumors can be dissipated by the energy from radiation (radiotherapy). Everything around us also emanates energy and crystals are unique in that the energy that radiates from them is stable and remains constant. Crystals are formed in patterns and structures which can be used to re-balance or re-tune our own energy fields.

While it is important to take professional medical advice if you suffer from any condition, throughout the ages, crystals have been used to heal and to maintain the balance of our own energy field. The raw energy contained in crystals is easy to attune to; it is formed from the same essential patterns that create all life in the universe. In crystal healing, specific qualities of different crystal structures are used to tune our own energy fields to their correct frequency. As with radiation (which is just light, after all) crystals can radiate energy that can help us to heal and also provide protection from ill-health.

Finding Your Crystals

Crystals have different qualities and even individual crystals of the same type will resonate differently on a very subtle level. Finding the right crystals for you is actually very easy – in fact the crystals will be more likely to find you! Simply holding a crystal in your hand will, with some practice, identify if it's the right crystal for you. In reality all crystals have beneficial qualities and as you start to work with crystals your choices can be more specific. Attuning yourself to crystals can take time – though for some individuals it is a faster process than for others. In this book we'll take you through some simple steps which will help on your journey including a close look at how to care for crystals and meditations to use when working with them.

If you have a very specific issue which you wish to address with crystals then finding an appropriate crystal which has links to that condition will be useful. However, intuition plays a large part in crystal healing and simply holding a crystal in your hand can often indicate if it is the right crystal for you. In this book we'll also take a look at some of the most popular crystals and their uses but always look to your reaction to a crystal to decide whether it can benefit you in anyway.

Crystals and the Chakras

Crystal healing is strongly associated with the concept of Chakras. These are traditional "energy" points identified in a number of healing systems, particularly those with roots in India and the Far East. The Chakras are understood as spinning, energy vortexes where our own individual energy field connects to the wider universe and to the greater energy that flows through it. Crystals are used for their own very strong qualities at focusing this energy to direct it into relevant energy points within the body and they can balance or stimulate the individual Chakras. For those new to energy healing, the recipe for success is simple; to address specific issues identify the Chakra that controls the particular bodily functions (or emotions) with which there is a problem and then use the crystals associated with the same conditions or energy. The seven primary Chakras are as follows;

1. The Base Chakra, or the Root Chakra is located at the base of the spine. This is related to physicality, grounding and a sense of belonging. It is associated with the color red and with our basic physical needs such as food and shelter.

2. Colored Orange, the Sacral Chakra is located a couple of inches below the navel and is linked to our relations with others, including romantic and sexual relationships. This Chakra is related to emotional issues, sexuality and our ability to experience pleasure.

3. The Solar Plexus Chakra, colored yellow is located in the upper portion of the abdomen around the stomach. This chakra relates to our sense of self, to confidence and our ability to be open and honest.

4. The Heart Chakra, colored green, is located in the center of our chest around the heart itself. It relates to our ability to love in the wider sense, our sense of respect for those around us and our ability to give of ourselves. The chakra governs health issues related to stress and to physical issues related to both the heart and lungs.

5. The Throat Chakra, colored blue, is located around our throats! It is related to communication, expression and creativity. Physically it can relate to throat and breathing issues, colds and flu.

6. The Third Eye Chakra, colored indigo, is located between the eyes on the forehead. This chakra is linked to wisdom, intuition and to decision making. It is related to mental issues and anxiety disorders including a range of depressive illnesses.

7. The Crown Chakra; this chakra is colored violet (although considered to be

colorless by some). It is located at the very top of our head. This chakra is related to spirituality, to bliss and to a connection with the wider universal forces. Illnesses including Alzheimer's, headaches, dizziness, depression and more serious mental illnesses such as schizophrenia are linked with this chakra.

Colors and Crystals

Colors have strong magical and healing associations in their own right and can be found playing a role in many different magical traditions from candle magic to chakra healing. The basic associations with each color are relevant in crystal healing as well, and these are described below:

• Red; signifies both fire and blood and is associated with both anger and focus. Passion, action and purification are also strongly associated with the color. Achieving grace through purification is also strongly linked to this color and it has powerful associations with radical change and healing.

• Orange; this color indicates spirituality, bravery, inspirational spontaneity, sociability, intelligence and contentment. Achieving balance and harmony in life is a strong feature of the associations with this color and it can be beneficial at establishing a sense of contentment.

• Yellow; a very individual color, yellow signifies creativity, focus, inspiration, ingenuity and inventiveness. It is associated with the sun, for obvious reasons, and was the imperial color in China where garments of yellow were worn by the Emperor alone. It

is associated strongly with authority, power and strength.

• Green; this color has many complex associations and it's the color that we see all around us. It symbolizes the earth, fertility and, in many cultures, has strong associations with the concept of the divine. Benevolence, temperance and empathy are common associations with this color and it is also strongly associated with good luck.

• Blue; the color of the heavens and the oceans, blue represent tranquility, peace, rest, recovery and good health. Associations with the sky mean that it linked to the element of air and to clarity of thought, while associations with oceans link it to emotions and particularly to serenity and peace.

• Indigo; a deeper form of blue, this color is associated with many similar attributes to that of blue but on a deeper level. Deep intellectual thought, serenity and peace of mind on the deepest level are all associations that come with this color. Wisdom and intuition are both strongly associated with indigo, as is the concept of justice.

• Violet; abundance, good fortune, plenty and leadership qualities are often associated with this color. In the west it was the color of emperors (as with yellow in the east) and many perceive this color to have similar connotations for this reason. Wealth and power are often associated with violet.

• White; a complex color that is associated with both clarity and purity but also with coldness and distance. White is, in fact, the absence of color and has associations with completion, the beginning and ends of cycles in all areas of life. It is the color of virginity, or youth, yet it is also the color of mourning, in many cultures, signifying death, old age and loss.

• Black; like white, this is another complex color with many associations. Again, used in mourning, it can also be associated with strength, prudence, wisdom and loyalty. Black is also the color of night and this creates associations with both magic and dreams along with intuitive knowledge and hidden knowledge.

Crystal Care and Cleaning

Crystals vibrate with energy and they can also store energy from all around them. They are not discriminating when it comes to absorbing vibrations and will pick up both positive and negative energies from the environment in which they are placed. For this reason it's important to take good care of your crystals and to ensure that they remain filled with positive, healing energy. Cleansing a crystal and "programming" it is a simple process and can be done in a number of ways. The two most common ways use water to help clean away negative vibrations. Some practitioners recommend using spring water (which is ideal) but a basic cleanse can be completed using running water of any kind (including from a tap!).

Below are three common methods used to cleanse crystals.

1. Hold your stone under a source of running water; this can be a stream or tap,

or water poured from a bottle or jug. Only use cold or slightly warm water, never hot. As the water flows over the stone simply visualize the negative energy and vibrations flowing away from the crystal and pure, positive energies flowing from your body into the stone. Do not dry using a towel or cloth but leave to dry naturally in the sun.

2. Place a bowl of water on a windowsill and add sea-salt giving it a good stir to ensure the salt is dissolved. Place your crystal in the bowl making sure that it is completely covered with water. Ideally do this at the start of the day as the sun rises and leave until midday when the sun is at its full height. Then remove the crystal and dry in the sunlight, as mentioned in the first method.

3. For quartz crystals, in particular, simply burying them in the earth is recommended by many practitioners. The planet itself is made up of approximately one third quartz and the magnetic energy

fields that this creates will help to cleanse your crystals in the most natural way. This both cleans and energizes your crystals. This method can be used for any crystal but is most effective for quartz of all kinds.

Programming Crystals

Crystal healing and meditation works by using the crystal's ability to store and focus energy. Crystals naturally pick up vibrations from around them but by programming your crystals you can focus the crystal's energy on a particular purpose. Once you have programmed a particular crystal the programming will remain and the energy that the crystal emits will continue to provide focus on the matter in question.

If you wish, you can "clear" this programming and/or "reprogram" the crystal as desired. Stones can be used for any purpose, for healing or protection, for luck, for love or for financial gain.

As each type of precious or semi-precious stone has different associations you should choose the most appropriate stone for your specific goal. Before you program a stone, or stones, you must be careful to clearly define your goal and the purpose for which you wish the stone to work. Properly programmed a crystal will be focused and powerful but clarity is crucial; remember that the stone cannot "think" for itself, if you are not sure of your own intention then this uncertainty will be fed into the stone!

To focus your thoughts simply think through what you require from the stone and write down this intention in a single sentence. Keep the sentence as short as possible with only one main point. Once you have this thought clearly in your mind you can begin to program your crystal.

Simply sit in a quiet space where you will not be interrupted and hold the stone in your hand (use your left hand if you are left handed or right if right handed). Some people like to burn an incense associated with the same purpose with which they wish to program the stone but, at first, it may be better to limit the distractions around you.

Focus on the stone, study it and feel its weight in your hand. Allow yourself to sense its energy, vibration and power. Gradually you will begin to feel a sense of harmony with the stone as it attunes to your energy and you to its. At this point the stone is ready to be programmed.

Deepen your focus on the stone and say out loud what purpose you wish the stone to fulfill. You can use your written statement if you wish and repeat this several times as you continue to focus on the crystal in your palm. Remain sitting quietly for a moment or two, still focused on the crystal and the thought with which you are programming it. Feel the energy in the crystal pulsing in your hand and imagine the outcome that you wish to achieve.

Once the stone is programmed it will retain the energy you have placed into it. You may wish to place the stone under your pillow or either carry it with you or place it in a specific location in your home. Crystals can pass their energy into other crystals if they touch, so you may wish to wrap the crystal in plain cloth to ensure that messages, energies and intentions don't become mixed. If this does happen by accident you'll need to cleanse your stones as described above and then reprogram them.

Chapter 11: Numerology Positions, Patterns, And Formulas

All patterns can be worked through in a lifetime. The numbers are simply a marker that point you in the right direction and give you hints as to what attributes you naturally possess. Depending upon where the number is positioned in the reading indicates how this number's pattern and meaning effect you.

Date of Birth
The birthdate is the starting point.

Example: 1/15/1954

Soul Number

The Soul Number is the day. Any number over 11 will need to be reduced. This is done by adding the two numbers together.

Example: 15 becomes 1+5=6

The Soul Number for 1/15/1954 is 6.

Soul Number Position

The Soul Number indicates where you were and what you were feeling in the last lifetime; what type of experiences you were having; what you are carrying from that last lifetime into the present; and both its skills and challenges.

Karmic Number

The Karma Number is the month. If it is December, reduce. This is done by adding the two numbers together. Example: 12 becomes 1+2 = 3

The Karma Number for 12/15/1954 is 3.

Karmic Number Position

The Karma Number indicates what the karmic challenges are in this lifetime; what you came in to learn; and what you are still working on. This position shows where you will be required to extend a tremendous effort throughout this life.

Gift Number

The Gift Number is the last two digits of the year. Any number over 11 will need to be reduced by adding them together.

Example: 54 becomes 5+4 = 9

The Gift Number for 1/15/1954 is 9.

Gift Number Position

The number in this position indicates where you have tremendous gifts and skills from many lifetimes of work; where you have naturally been drawn to show up and assist; your natural skills; and what you love to do. This gift is easy to share with others.

Path Number

The Path Number is found by adding all four digits of the year together and then reduce if necessary. Example: 1+9+5+4 = 19 then 1+9 = 10

The Path Number for 1/15/1954 is 10.

Path Number Position

The Path Number shows what the path of this life will look like; how karma may present itself; directs toward the completion of the karma; how you will handle the challenges; and how to proceed.

Destiny Number

The Destiny Number is found by adding together all the numbers of the birthdate and reduce if necessary. Example: 1+1+5+1+9+5+4 = 26; then 2+6 =8

The Destiny Number for 1/15/1954 is 8.

Destiny Number Position

The Destiny Number indicates what your ultimate goal is in this lifetime; where you intend to be when you are past the age of 35. When the Destiny Number is completed then new doors open into realities that you could not have previously conceived. This is because you will have stepped beyond the karmic lessons of this life, walked the path to your destiny and are now free to become whoever and whatever you choose.

Year Number

The year number is calculated by adding the digits of the month and the day of the birthdate with the four digits of the present year. Reduce if over 11. The example is for 2005.
Example: 1+1+5+2+0+0+5 = 14 then 1+4 = 5

The year number is 5.

Year Number Position

The year number tells you what the pattern will be for the year beginning at your birthday and ending at the following birthday. The year number hints at possible problems and issues that might arise during that time. How you handle the situations will give you insight and growth into the energies that affect you for that year. Knowing what may arise allows you to anticipate and plan ahead. This allows the transcendence of personal struggle and suffering into conscious clarity.

Corresponding Number Associated With Planetary Positions

The thirteen moon cycles, the twelve signs of the zodiac, and the eleven numbers in numerology all work together. Each number is associated with a planet based upon the astrological position of our present day calendar system. The trick is that number systems were created before our modern calendar and the invention of astrology. Because of this, we need to sort out the different systems in order to understand and connect them. Let us start with some history.

In ancient times, the seasons were based on the cycles of the moon, thus giving the ancient calendars thirteen cycles in relationship to the phases of the moon. (There are thirteen moon cycles per year.)

Astrology has twelve different signs in the Zodiac. Because the astrologers could not see beyond our solar system, they overlapped the planet Mercury as being aligned with Gemini and Virgo, and they overlapped the planet Venus with Taurus and Libra.

In Numerology there are only eleven numbers because we count the modern astrological planet of Chiron as a planet. This turns the month of May into the archetype of Chiron. Turns the planet of Venus from Taurus to Chiron. This still causes the 12th month, December, to revert to the 3 position (12, 1+2=3) and is translated back to the position of Neptune. Therefore the month of March and the month of December will be translated through two levels of the planet of Neptune. The distinction is the flavor of the corresponding astrological sign, for each will subtly shade the interpretation.

As an example; the Neptunian experience for a Pisces would be that they are looking for perfection (the Karma of 3 vibration), from the standpoint of needing to complete karmic lessons by reframing them to a positive. Pisces are attempting to finish up all karma within the time period of being Pisces. Pisces are like a salmon constantly swimming upstream and they must get past all the obstacles along the way in order to be complete. This translates into needing to see all challenges as positive and overcome all negative and negating beliefs about themselves and the situations in which they find themselves.

On the other hand, Sagittarius is looking to find perfectionism (the Karma of 3 vibration) by wanting to be in the right place at the right time. Sagittarius is naturally positive and exuberant, yet the grass always seems greener on the other side. Sagittarians are searching for total inner wisdom and knowing. The conflict with perfectionism comes in because they lack staying power on projects. They begin new ones before they are completed with the old ones. This causes them to feel as if they are not reaching their perfect potential. If they are not willing to learn the lesson of emotional depth and follow through which is Neptune then they will have a life of missed deadlines, unfinished projects and shallow emotional commitments.

This same situation shows up again in Numerology because the number ten is translated as the planet of Jupiter and the astrological sign of Libra rather than its traditional astrological position of Sagittarius. Jupiter traditionally belongs to Sagittarius but in numerology we translate it to become associated with Libra. Therefore the karma of a Libra or early Scorpio (meaning those born on the month of October), will be working on the karma of power and influence.

In dealing with the numbers as they relate to astrology, remember that the astrological information is most easily translated through the karmic position. Meaning that this planetary and astrological position is what you are working on in this lifetime. This will be where the struggles are played out, and how you learn to deal with these challenges determines the successes and failures in your life.

These karmic associations help to see the subtle balances and trends of each person. However, where the number shows up is an indication of the astrological planet and sign and aids in understanding and interpreting the number and position. If you have a dominance of a particular number over and over again in your numerological patterns, then this energy or type influences and colors your perceptions and behaviors. It will often indicate how you appear to others and explain why people might respond in a particular way.

As an example; someone who has a lot of 3's in their numbers is going to come across as a Neptunian/Piscean person in how they approach life. The same is true with the other numbers.

This becomes more interesting because in astrology the last few days of the year are often associated with the upcoming astrological sign. Example: 1-15-1954 is Capricorn and 1-25-1954 is Aquarius. This causes this Aquarius to have the karmic pattern that is associated with Capricorn rather than Aquarius. (This person may have learned the lessons of Aquarius and the karma number of two).

The 1-25-1954 pattern indicates that the person in this position has probably been in this particular sign in another lifetime. He wants to do this astrological pattern again but now has a different karmic lesson than the typical sign that he was born into.

The person born 1-25-1954 therefore is an Aquarius with the karma of a Capricorn. The number one and the planet Saturn rule the karma of a Capricorn. Saturn is the planet of hard work and struggle and this shows that this Aquarius must be willing to work hard for what he believes in order to succeed. Yet he does not have the typical karma of a two for the month of February, as he was not born in February. Most Aquarians are born in the month of February and only a few are born in the month of January. The karma of 2 (February) is about learning critical mind and exploring consciousness through understanding duality. But in our example, this Aquarian is going to be driven karmically like a Capricorn and be less critical and mental than a typical Aquarian. He will have the fortitude and staying power of Saturn, the planet of hard work and struggle. He will tend to be more financially successful then the Aquarian energy of two.

The same will be true of all the astrological patterns. In another example: If someone is a Virgo born in the end of August rather than born typically in September, she will have the karma of a Leo. The karma of Leo is the karma of sadness and grief. This means that she is holding inner sadness from other lifetimes and is attempting to let go of it. The typical karma of a Virgo is the number nine. This karma is about exploring the emotional body, mysticism, and art. So a person born 8-27-45 is a Virgo that has already done the karma of nine and she wants to do Virgo again, but she comes across as a Leo outwardly. This can show a more dynamic Virgo that is sunny and outgoing in her personality, yet afraid to show her inner pain and sadness. Typical Virgos who are born in September can be more emotional, deep, withdrawn, and detail-oriented.

Chapter 12: The Magician

The picture is depicted by a confident young magician who stands with an infinite symbol on his head signifying unlimited confidence in him. He wears a snake around his waist that is swallowing its own tail symbolizing eternity. The magician holds a wand with his right hand pointing to the infinite intelligence and his left hand pointing to mother earth signifying that he has the power to unite the primal and sublime energies. The red robe and red roses signify his qualities of passion and ardent desire. The white lilies suggest purity of thought. On the table in front of the Magician are the symbols of the four Tarot suits implying that the Magician can perform miracles if he learns the technique of perfectly controlling the four elements of nature namely the fire, water, air and earth with passion and purity of thought.

Those who fall under the influence of this card are eloquent and charismatic. Both verbally and in writing, they are clever, witty, inventive and persuasive. Career accomplishments play a vital role in the natives' lives. These people are gifted with great persuasive power that can convince people of almost anything. For better or worse, their words are magic. These passionate, artistic, creative, insightful and devoted individuals will excel if they chose to be in the world of arts or other creative areas. However, the natives should exercise caution in being over-confident, superficial, disorganized, deceitful or egoistic behavior as these traits may lead to their downfall.

Winston Churchill

Key Compound Number = 1

Sir Winston Churchill is the hero of the Second World War. He is widely regarded as one of the greatest wartime leaders of the century and served as British Prime Minister. A noted statesman and orator, Churchill was also an officer in the British Army, a historian, a writer, and an artist. He is the only British Prime Minister to have received the Nobel Prize in Literature Winston Churchill has 27 vowels that brings in strife and struggles. As a young army officer, he saw action in British India, the Sudan and the Second Boer War. He gained fame as a war correspondent. The 55 consonants brought his victories and long lasting fame. He was born on 30 November that makes a Sagittarius with a strong sense of independence. His destiny number 61 (30+11+1+8+7+4 = 61) promises success through craft. And 61 reduced to the base number 7 makes him the Charioteer. He was indeed a charioteer of the Second World War who led Britain's victory over Nazi Germany. Churchill is widely regarded as being among the most influential persons in British history. This great leader, statesman, orator and writer are a true Magician.

THE HIGH PRIESTESS

The High Priestess is also called the Goddess of Underworld. She has a lunar crescent at her feet and a crown in the shape of a pomegranate flower. The scroll in her hands is inscribed with the word 'Tora', signifying the Greater Law or the

Secret Law. It is partly covered by her gown, to show that some things are implied and some spoken. She is seated between the white and black pillars 'J' and 'B' of a mystic Temple and the veil is embroidered with palms and pomegranates. She is aware of the extreme opposites, and knows both sides of a situation. Hence, she finds it difficult to make choices. The High Priestess is a repository of knowledge, a walking library with uncanny instincts and insights. She is usually interpreted as a spiritual woman, a nun or astrologer, a teacher of archaic knowledge, or just someone who knows many secrets. Those who fall under the influence of this number make good teachers, artists, inventors, mediators, peace makers or diplomats. These people are not persuasive individuals and often prefer to stay in the background. They can be of great service to others because of their ability to settle things amicably and the natives may well become the power behind the throne. However the natives should make sure to be insensitive or over sensitive and get depressed if their surroundings are

Martin Luther King

Key Compound Number = 2

Martin Luther King was an American clergyman, activist, and prominent leader in the African American civil rights movement who was inspired by Gandhi's non-violent activism. His main legacy was securing progress on civil rights in the United States. Because of this work, he has become a human rights icon. He raised public consciousness of the civil rights movement and incidentally established himself as one of the greatest orators in U.S. history. King was the youngest person to receive the Nobel Peace Prize for his work to end racial segregation and racial discrimination through civil disobedience and other non-violent means. By the time of his death in 1968, he had refocused his efforts on ending poverty and the Vietnam War. King's popular "I Have a Dream" speech has inspired Barack Obama to become the first African American President of the United States. King was assassinated and this untimely death is due to 16 alphabets in his name.

THE EMPRESS

The Empress card is illustrated by a royal lady in rich ornaments and royal aspect, as of a daughter of heaven and earth. Though number 3 is ruled by Jupiter, her tiara has twelve stars, gathered in a cluster. The symbol of Venus is on the shield which rests near her. A field of wheat is ripening in front of her, and there is a waterfall in the background. The scepter which she bears is surmounted by the globe of this world symbolizing authoritative position. The Empress is a creator, be it creation of life, of romance, of art, of business or empires.

People under the influence of this number are extremely expressive and possess the art of conversation. These people influence others through their ability to communicate about life in a grandiose fashion and love to travel a lot. Recognition is very important to them and these people like to be appreciated. The natives are very good in speculation.

Growth and expansion in all spheres of their life is guaranteed. On the lower octave, though these people are very caring, they worry over petty things. They should know when to let go. It is important to realize that even plants can die from over-watering as easily as neglect. Most of all, like any pregnant mother or good gardener, they have exercise patience. All things need time to gestate and sprout.

Sun Yat-sen

Key Compound Number = 3

Sun Yat-sen was a Chinese revolutionary and president. As the foremost pioneer of Nationalist China, Sun is referred to as the "Father of the Nation" in the Republic of China (ROC), and the "forerunner of democratic revolution" in the People's Republic of China. Sun played an instrumental role in the overthrow of the Qing dynasty during the Xinhai Revolution. Sun was the first provisional president when the Republic of China was founded in 1912 and later co-founded the Kuomintang (KMT), serving as its first leader. Sun was a uniting figure in post-Imperial China, and remains unique among 20th century Chinese politicians for being widely revered amongst the people from both sides of the Taiwan Strait.

THE EMPEROR

The Rebel Emperor is seated on a solid stone throne decorated with Ram's heads symbolizing Aires, the first sign of the Zodiac. Like an infant, he is filled with enthusiasm, energy and aggression. The powerful and authoritative figure in this card is clearly the master of his own destiny. He is straight forward, naive, honest and quite often irresistible. His very way of being rebellious is not because he is fighting against anybody or anything, but because he has discovered his own true nature and is determined to live in accordance with it. The Emperor holds a scepter in one hand implying that he is the authority figure. In the best state of affairs, he signifies the leader that everyone wants to follow; sitting on a throne that indicates the solid foundation of an Empire he has created, he rules with rational thought and enthusiasm. His grey beard implies that he has obtained his wisdom through experience that makes him an excellent source of advice. He does not get carried away by fad or fancy and nothing slips by his scrutiny. The Emperor is a master of his own making and realizes his inner strength that makes him a true leader. However, on the lower octave, those who fall under the influence of this card should try to let go off being manipulative and overly critical. These people should learn to release the need to control everything. The natives must realize that what is best for them may not necessarily make them feel good. The natives can also be rebellious, impatient, annoying, demanding and controlling just like a baby. These people should always try to seek a sense of balance between love and power in order to lead a peaceful life.

Julius Caesar

Key Compound Number - 4

Julius Caesar was a Roman military and political leader. He played a critical role in the transformation of the Roman Republic into the Roman Empire. As a politician, Caesar made use of popular tactics. He formed political alliances in order to dominate Roman politics. Caesar's conquest of Gaul extended the Roman world to the North Sea, and he

also conducted the first Roman invasion of Britain. These achievements granted him unmatched military power and Caesar emerged as the unrivalled leader of the Roman world by 49 B.C.

After assuming control of government, he began extensive reforms of Roman society and government. He centralized the bureaucracy of the Republic and was eventually proclaimed "dictator in perpetuity". A group of senators, led by Marcus Brutus, assassinated the dictator, hoping to restore the normal running of the Republic. However, the result was a series of civil wars, which ultimately led to the establishment of the permanent Roman Empire by Caesar's adopted heir Augustus.

Chapter 13: The Vedic Influence On Numbers

Astronomy and Astrology (Jyotisha) are components of the great Vedas and being their anga (part), Vedic study cannot be complete without a study of these two components. Jyotisha is intended to be helpful to the individual in that it shows his/her limitations and defects, and if one profits by its advice, he/she can be more composed and peaceful, instead of running after mirages.

Many of the ideas of modern astronomy and astrology can be traced back to the Asya Vamasya Sukta (compilation), Rigveda 1–164 of Dirghatamas.

Great astrologers and thinkers like Viscount Cheiro, Count Bjcostjernemons and Alice Bailey concluded that these Hindu sciences co-evolved with the Hebrew scriptures.

Viscount Cheiro, who connected all the verses of the Bhishmapurna from the Mahabharata and put them in his famous book, **Cheiro's Numerology**, said that "we must not forget that it was the Hindus who disclosed what is known as the procession of the equinoxes and in their calculations, such an occurrence takes place every 25,827 years." [**Cheiro's Book of Numbers**, Page 19]

The ancient Indian astronomer, Aryabhatta, long before Copernicus, maintained that the earth moved around the sun! Another astronomer, Soumaka, gave the distance of the sun from the earth, which is surprisingly close to modern estimates. Bhaskaracharya regarded the earth as suspended in space centuries before Newton. The Dirghatamas disclosed the rotations and space solar sidereal computations 5,000 years before Einstein!

To better appreciate the magnitude of such an ancient civilisation like India and its wisdom, here's a brief insight into the Vedas for you readers. The four Vedas, Rigveda, Yajurveda, Samaveda and Atharvaveda, formed the core of the Hindu religion. To these were added four more:

Ayurveda — the science of life

Arthashastra — the science of wealth and economics

Dhanurveda — the science relating to weaponry, missiles and warfare

Gandharvaveda — treatises on the fine arts such as music, dance and drama

There are also the Vedaangas, which are auxiliaries to the Vedas, namely,

Siksha (euphony and pronounciation), Vyaakarna (grammar), Chandas (metre), Niruktha (etymology), Jyotisha (astronomy/astrology), Kalpa (procedure), and Meemamsa (interpretation of vedic texts).

The Vedas are called Anaadi — which means without a beginning in terms of time. That is, anything previous to them or older than them does not exist.

So, they have existed at all times. A book has necessarily to have an author, at least one if not more — such as the Old Testament, which is a collection of the sayings of many saints. The Koran contains what Prophet Mohammed propagated. Buddhists have the Dhammapada. Parsis have the Zend Avesta.

All these books were by people who existed at some point of time. Before them, their teachings were not available. On the contrary, the Vedas were conveyed by Gurus to disciples and no texts were available.

As for numerology, there is evidence of only one scripture that has been passed down generation to generation, but there are no details yet available about this. This is in the **Vasudevananda Saptasathi**, written by Rangavadhoot in the year 1818. Here, in Chapter 28, titled Kardamaprajapati, it is mentioned in the third and fourth shlokas that the wife of Kardama, named Devahooti, had delivered a son named Kapila, assumed to be the incarnation of Lord Vishnu (one of the trinity of Brahma-Vishnu-Shiva) and the one who wrote the **Sankyashastra** on numerology.

Chapter 14: Your Social Attributes

Numbers are the basic causes that influence shape and rejuvenate your life trends. All the aspects of our personality are influenced by Planetary Numbers 1 to 9.Our social status too is influenced as well by these Divine Numbers.

Some persons are very magnetic n command great social respect; some enjoy assertive status; some are not able to influence people much n some are noticed too much and their presence means a lot to those around them.

Let us see relevance of Planetary Numbers 1 to 9 on your social attributes, image and status that you enjoy in society.

Number 1

Persons endowed with Birth Number 1 have boon of high intellectual level, management abilities n reasoning skills. They are born leaders n know how to assert themselves. Hence, they outshine in their social circle and are most willing to help needy people, due to their benevolent nature. People are easily convinced with their logic. But, at times, gossip mongers try to defame them out of jealousy.

Number 2

Persons bestowed with Number 2 are gifted with all rounder personality .They have a very adjusting temperament, keen aesthetic and creative skills. They like socializing and have lots of friends. But many a times, they are easily exploited and their emotions are misused.

Number 3

Persons bestowed with Number 3 are master minds, are interested in academic, literary, social and creative pursuits. They assume domestic, professional and social liabilities willingly and are able to discharge their liabilities in an influential manner, hence, their recognition in society is greater and command respect and love.

Number 4

Persons endowed with Number 4 are untraditional in their view, have innovative n calculative mind. Management skills and leadership attributes bring them to forefront in society. Due to their habit of indulgence in arguments and being outspoken, they sometime face defamation.

Number 5

Persons endowed with Number 5 are independent in nature n are able to take decisions on their own. They have management skills, calculative mind and are gifted with intuition. They assume social n domestic responsibilities willingly and have unending zeal. So, they are popular in society.

Number 6

Persons bestowed with Number 6 have a magnetic personality, keen aesthetic sense and carry the day where ever they go. They are good in social interaction and enjoy popularity. They love to spend time with family and for socializing too.

Number 7

Persons bestowed with Number 7 have deep aesthetic sense, an adjusting temperament and multi faceted personality, but don't share their hearts easily. They love to spend time with family and friends, but are quite introvert at times.

Number 8

Persons bestowed with Number 8 are well defined in their attributes, firm minded and capable of acting independently. At times, they turn arrogant and egoistic. They are not very popular in social circle. But, if you want to rely on them for support, they will surely help you to tackle the problems.

Number 9

Persons bestowed with Number 9 have virtue of self reliance, independent personality and a mature mind. They don't easily mix up with each and every person around them, but they believe in depth of relations. They are reliable.

Chapter 15: The Basic Numerology Chart

You have understood what numerology is and have also understood the science behind numerology. I will now take you through the numerology chart and give you a detailed explanation of what you will need to know while reading a person's chart.

The chart

When you look at a numerology chart, you will find numbers that have been explained to you as well. This should never surprise you since you will be able to understand the numbers better. But, there are people all over the world who have gained a tremendous insight into what these numbers may mean to them on their own by experiencing the approach mentioned on the chart.

You will be able to learn through a different approach in this chapter. This approach is based on the idea that the chart has been made of functional elements that have been based on the three core elements. It also helps you understand what it is that you can do in your life with the knowledge of these core elements. You will be able to understand the traits of a person as well!

Thoughts, obstacles and the law of attraction

Every obstacle that stands in the way of your success and your happiness always exists only in your mind. This will always make you want to focus on these objects. What you forget is that the more you focus on these objects, the more power you are giving them to manifest themselves into your world. This is because of the fact that thoughts are always what you want most. What was not mentioned earlier was that these thoughts always feed on your emotions and will grow with your thoughts. This is the exact way the law of attraction works. It is also the same reason why you find yourself in a situation where you would rather never be in although you have tried so hard to avoid the situation!

The greatest news here is that the mind can always be changed. It is because of this that you can change the way you connect with your core elements and will find yourself being able to change the pattern of your vibrations. You will be able to learn quickly about the attitudes and ideas you must have in order to understand the state of wellness and success. You will also be able to understand relationships better through a change in the way you think. These are not based on any cosmic laws. The only laws that you will need to worry about are the ones that are hell bent on getting you what you want most and the ones that deal with projecting every thought that you experience.

The core elements

The three core elements of your numerological chart are the life path, the soul urge and the expression. These three are extremely important since they show a great deal of information about the nature of yourself and will also help in projecting your inborn qualities to the people around you. These are what create your destiny.

The next few chapters leave you with a great deal of information on how the core elements work. You will also see how these core elements will help you make certain changes in your life, which would create a positive impact on your life. Before getting into this, you will have to know what the numbers means individually. You will need to understand how you can interpret the numbers. You need to remember that the way you interpret the number depends only on how you perceive the number.

The numbers are what make numerological charts personal since each person has a number that exudes a certain vibration. These numbers always act differently and always work with the elements of the numerological chart. Before you understand what the numbers are, let us delve into the core elements and see how you can make the changes you desire to see in you! In order to help you understand the core elements better, we would need to consider a birthday. Let us consider the birthday September 5th, 1993.

Chapter 16: Karmic Debt Numbers (Kdn):

Karmic Debt Numbers (KDN) are 4 sets of numbers in the numerological spectrum, which contain high intensity of past Karmic actions, the results of which these people still feel in their present lives. It is certainly beneficial to know how these people are affected by these numbers and how they can come out from their unique challenges. If not these KDN can cloud the vibrations of their life path and they will not see the blossoming benefits even if they are a master number.

The KDN are 13, 14, 16 and 19 and as long as they surface in a person's five core numbers including the pinnacle and life goal numbers he/she have to pay careful attention to the ill-effects these numbers can bring about. The emotional, Spiritual and Karmic residue these unique numbers contain express themselves in their unique manner. By studying them you will know, why these people behave peculiarly to meet the similarities and familiarities of such persistent challenges.

These KDN people are SPECIAL, because they are the blessed and chosen people, who when they overcome their challenges, can become better evolved with SPECIAL POWERS and that makes them superior to others.

a) KARMIC DEBT NUMBER 13: these people basically face failures often that is their mantra to overcome and be strengthened. They must not become disenchanted and as failures are the learning and launching pad to climb up the ladder of success. KDN 13people face many obstructions

KDN 13 people tend to meet with innumerable failures. All these are the Karmic residual consequences of their past self-centered actions. I remember Simon Yeo who was born on 13.2.1974 is a KDN 13. As a child he faced many failures especially not doing well in his studies. He was a failure in both English and Mathematics. He did not make the great to be in his school's soccer team. He was at first disappointed and was also to take failures as a stepping stone before success and finally he started passing his English and Mathematics. He trained hard and became the school's soccer team's Captain. Initially they can ONLY see the steps like steeps and rungs like wrongs. But PERSEAVENCE, ENSURE to wriggle from the struggles.

In the case of Jean S Scully, she was initially a teacher, a single mother and with just a secondary education, she was too short for a modelling career, she was dependent and even took up drugs and her mother Tabitha was a hopeless alcoholic without a proper guide she became a single mother without a proper job and found her child to be a cumbersome thing. Once Jean even wrote on a piece of paper,

"I Only lure Failure, Failure, Failure

So Many Things Remain Unsure

So Much Pain I Endure

I am still finding the Cure."

This caught the eagle-eyes of her teacher who saw her potential in writing and she encouraged Jean to write. Her first book on the story of Scottish Whiskies was a mediocre success. But it make her feel good and made her write further. With new concepts publishers came and knocking on her main door willing even to pay up front a deposit for her books. It is clear for KDN 13 success is a reward that is attained after the initial struggles are they need persistence, dreams and discipline to succeed and must never give in to use unethical measures to be successful.

KARMIC DEBT NUMBER 14: The KDN 14 people may be submerged with total CRISIS in many parts of their lives (This is their Mantra). Which can overwhelmed them. Though each crisis can appear suddenly they when using their mental fortitude can overcome them and these experiences can shape them into battle-hardened people.

KDN 14 people doggerly attract movements of CRISIS in their Pinnacle Numbers. Hence the olympionic spirit to deal with such challenges will make them into better persons.

KDN 14 people have wrongly used their power and freedom in their previous lives and find themselves in the mire of sex, drugs, alcohol etc in their present lives. in the number 5 (1+4=5), they have the tendency to over-excessively indulge in vices and abuse their freedom in the negative ways with care and control they can reach their goals with discipline. They must set their lives in order and be committed in facing their unexpected challenges to procure what they want.

KARMIC DEBT NUMBER 16: These KDN 16 people will attract ILLUSIONS (This Their

Mantra). They go after things that were not meant for them after wasting much of their precious time. They will be miserable that these ventures were a waste of time and a wanton pursuit.

KDN 16 people though their lives are shackled with delusions and illusions. They must use these challenges as a transition point.

KDN 16 people have the vibrations of number 7 (1+6=7), REMUS ZHANG was born on 16.7.1972 and though he possessed his degree in Fashion and Design, he could not maintain a full-time job, as all his time was spent on girls, sex and alcohol. This was his only passion and his aim to do well in the fashion industry took a back seat. His progress in life was stunted until he went for a Christian detox camp which help him tremendously to contain, control and compress his vices. Now he has ensued his name as a much-sought after fashion designer in South-East Asia.

KDN 16(vibration 7) must be modest and subdue their ego and learn to respect other people and not always put their ideas and opinions as the main stream of their lives. They will not have many friends as they think very high of themselves, in terms of image and talents. They must calm their over-anxious minds. They seem to be eluded with what they can really do and most of the time they live in their own make-belief world. The best advice for these people...

Re: "You can fumble

You can even tremble

But if you not humble. Surely you will tumble"

KARMIC DEBT NUMBER 19: These KDN 19 people will face lot of SEPARATIONS (That is their Mantra). That could be in their relationships, in their friendship circles passed on loved ones or even separation from their goals and beliefs. But they need to surmount and circumvent them and NOT be over helmed by them.

KDN 19 people must change isolation and separation and configure them into a terrific transfiguration in their lives.

These numbers must not be taken lightly when they appear in person's five core number including the pinnacle and Life Goal numbers.

KDN 19 people will be alone and forced to be independent often from young. But this separation which coaches them independence is self-imposed. They strive to be on their own and shun all help from even well-meaning ones. As a number 1(1+9=10) they will not lend a listening ear and want to strike it out all on their own. They need to come to the realization that they need love and support from others. They need to listen and be attentive that others do care about them.

When I first came to know Jerelyn Juion Geables, who was born on 19.9.1981. She was a single mother, separated from her husband and was quite anti-social. Upon knowing her birth date it was clear that her karmic debt number that her past live is directly impacting her present one and with the help of her cousin Agnes Montinez, she began listening to people and started to have more friends and widened her social network. Today she is happily married to Edward, a businessman, running her own food catering business in Balabagoes Ilo Ilo, Philippines.

Karmic Debt Numbers can have a detrimental effect a person's education, carrier, marriage and relationships with people, as long as it appears in the FIVE core numbers of a person, namely a) Psychic Number, b) Life Path Number, c) Karmic Number, d) Secret Heart Desire Number and e) Outer Character Number. If left understand, subsequently I am giving those affected and effected by this KDN a way to mitigate the potency of these KDN. Please do the suggested mental exercise to obtain and realize the effects in this life time. If the KDN appear, as in the case of Hanvitha, who is born on 19.1.2015, she will feel the effect from birth, until her life path number takes over.

Rationale for Priya Yoga for Karmic Debt Numbers

In this process and exercise through visualization you are involving your concerted Karma of your past life and GIVING IT AWAY, like a philanthropist. In other words, it is a natural transparence, like a money transfer from your account to another one. Do this with the self-belief and it will work when done with your heart, soul, mind and spirit.

KARMIC DEBT NUMBERS SOLUTION/REMEDY/PANACEA

Though this not the last chapter of this book. It is candidly the last one, I am putting my thoughts to. That too after endless nights of sleeplessness which nearly drove me into dazed somnambulist. After much in research into the subject, and having head consulted a follower of the original Patanjali yoga sutra, I am propagating this unique magic method to contain, cure and consume the past Karma of those affected by KDN.

No doubt, cultivates in Karmic Debt Numbers (KDN) point to a hopeless conclusions of no return and NOTHING effectively can be done to from oneself, from the teaches of past Karma is action, thoughts, even in the mental abode: simply put – you reap what you sow. The basic of Karma in itself is a vast ocean but it is only torched on for the solo purpose of helping those affected by the karmic debt numbers.

It is a fallacy to surrender to the fatalist notion that nothing can be done once you are born with a KDN.

Those born on 13, 14, 16 and 19 or have these numbers on their FIVE core numerological charts can mitigate the effects of past karmic baggage by

Praying to whichever god they choose

Doing good deeds in their present lives

Using Priya (Love) yoga techniques, which is as follows

This should be done between 4.30am to 6.30am

Your environment should be devoid of noise and light

Sit comfortably

Breathe in to the count of 4 using your nostrils.

Hold that breathe to the count of 8

Exhale your held breath using BOTH your nostrils and your mouth to the count of 21. Repeat this breathing exercise atleast 8 times until you are in a relax mode.

With eyes closed imaging the Sun facing you, behind you is all total darkness. In front of you is light

In front of you is a row of people in a line and some of them you may recognize as those you have wronged.

You are holding a bag in your left hand. Using your right hand open the bag and give your karma from the bag to all those in the row until the bag is empty. Some may refuse to take but you must insist.

Give the empty bag to the last person in that row and in your mind you can think of a peson's name whom you have done much wrong to. That person give that empty bag, turn away from this people and walk towardsthe portion of total darkness and never, never look back.

Repeat this as often as you could and you will be amazed with the results.

Chapter 17: Entrepreneur, Accountant, Boss, Manager, Planner Heart Of The Accountant

Do people call you stubborn? Not if they want to stay on your good side. 4 is a masculine number for both men and women. 4s are strong-willed, even stubborn, and often the people the rest of us lean on for support and doing the hard, dirty work as well as the foundations of society. An emotionally balanced 4 is among the most dependable of the birthdays, but one out of sorts with himself or who is extremely insecure or overly concerned about "keeping up with the Jones." 4s prefer their personal world to be their way, preferably with all the proverbial ducks neatly lined up, and it drives them mad when those ducks get out of line. 4 symbolizes firmness, a steadfast character, what I loosely call an accountant's personality, but not necessarily an accountant as such (you should check the Birthday numbers of accountants who enjoy their work, or someone who truly enjoys working with figures), but someone who is more comfortable working with tangible things instead of theory. 4s need well-defined boundaries. As a rule, a 4 is most comfortable with anything he can touch, see, hear, feel or taste. In other words, the five senses. He sometimes ignores his sixth sense of intuition, especially if it fails him a few times. Their lifelong challenge is learning to trust their intuition and to let out their creativity. They prefer realism, but fantasy is the basis of creativity. 4's need for order and control makes them dependable, the best of planners or the best of conspirators. They enjoy putting plans into action. 4s pursue everything with a passion, whether it is taking charge or being couch potatoes. Their perfectionist nature is both their strong point and their undoing. 4s have the strong-minded nature and stamina to attain what they want. They need to make sure and not hold in their emotions. They often play their cards close to their chests. 4s are very physical and have tightly compacted energy that can break loose with a vengeance. A 4 adult is the individual who can be very proper at work, then wind up drunk and wearing a lampshade on his head at the office party.

The nodes of the moon are two artificial orbital points of the moon used for astrological reference. You 4 birthdays owe part of your nature to the North Node, which I often refer to by its Sanskrit name, Rahu. The North Node gives 4 Birthdays the stamina to strive and attain, as well as act stubbornly. 4 is a fixed number, and it strengthens a weaker sun sign it may accompany, such as Pisces or Libra. 4 gives its natives many masculine characteristics. I see a 4 Birthday as having the same strengthening effect on a person as having a Virgo or Scorpio sun sign or a strong influence from either of these in the astrological chart. Combine a 4 Birthday with a strong sun sign such as Aires, Taurus, Leo, Virgo or Scorpio, and you have one extremely powerful individual regardless of the rest of his chart.

The leaders of two nations whose political and financial philosophies changed the course of modern history, George Washington and Nikolai Lenin, were born on the 22nd, thus, were 22/4 Birthdays. The United States' greatest local nemesis, Fidel Castro, who in his better days, was a top notch schemer, is a 13 Birthday, also a 4. Robert Louis Stevenson, the author of **Dr. Jekyll and Mr. Hyde**, in which a respected physician turns himself into a raving madman through a serum he develops, was born on the 22nd. 4s are the cornerstone personalities, the guardians of societies and their values.

4s are not naturally materialistic, but they are security minded. 4's financial speculation should be kept to solid, secure investments with proven track records. As a rule, 4s are steady employees and hard workers. These are people who do well being self-employed. Since they prefer dealing with tangibility, they do well in banking, real estate, or the production end of any business. When I did readings at realtor and banker parties during that time period, there were many 4s in attendance. They are happiest in jobs where they can see the results of their labor. They are hands-on people and make good supervisors who work side by side with those they supervise. They are not as happy being in the more removed position of company director or CEO, unless they own the company.

The Mexican revolutionary leader who eluded capture by the U.S. Cavalry, Poncho Villa, was born on the 4th. He always rode into battle with his troops. He definitely was hands on, worked side by side with his "employees" and was the CEO. Again, Fidel Castro, who was born on August 13th, is a prime contemporary example of the 4's hands-on managerial style as he commanded a company of troops during the Bay of Pigs invasion, as well as being a forceful dictator. During his younger years, he occasionally worked alongside farm workers harvesting sugar cane. The late yuppie activist, Jerry Rubin, claimed that Castro's action was the most ideal example of Socialist leadership. I say it was an example of the 4's need for hands-on supervision. Had Castro remained in his war room, he would have choked at the bit during the entire episode. In an interview during the 1970s, Castro admitted to having pushed the button that fired a missile that shot down an American spy plane. During his younger years, he also worked alongside his fellow Cubans with the sugarcane harvest. Castro also is the prime contemporary example that as political leaders, 4s easily can become dictatorial but defend against any outside attempt to take control away from them. This tight control extends into the classroom of any 4 teacher. They are firm teachers who sincerely care for their students but whose students consider them hard-nosed.

4 children need a strong outlet for this energy, less they wind up bullies. Even as adults, they are very physical and need regular exercise or any regular outlet for letting emotions loose. A 4 Birthday is beneficial for professional athletes, especially in the more violent sports. During the 1930's, Adolph Hitler and Nazi Germany's propaganda machine preached Aryan Supremacy. Joe Louis, the late Black World Heavyweight boxing champion, was born on the 13th. He embarrassed Nazi Germany's propaganda of Aryan Supremacy by soundly defeating Germany's champion, Max Schmeling. Another pioneer for black athletes was

Jackie Robinson, born on the 31st. As a university student, Fidel Castro excelled at baseball enough to gain the attention of the Washington Senators who sent out a scout to watch him in action. A good example of the physical nature of the 4 occurred one night when I was sitting in a bar where there was a widescreen television. The woman bartender, a very serious 22/4 Birthday, was flipping the channels and passed a cable station movie in which a young woman was being spanked. Several men at the bar said they wanted to watch one or another of the sports channels, but the woman insisted that she wanted to see someone getting spanked. In such a situation, the 4 prefers being on the giving end, rather than the receiving. This strongly physical nature is greatly enhanced by a 4, 8, or 9 Façade number. A 1 Façade would not be misleading to strangers because both 1 and 4 are very independent.

Creatively, 4s tend to be the motley crew of numbers. 4s do best working with the tangible, more grounded aspects instead of abstract theory, except the 13th or the 31st, whose solid 4 trademark remains but leans more to the creative end of the 4 spectrum. Not that a 4 isn't creative, but as with any other sort of work, the 4 prefers realism to fantasy and fantasy is the basis of any creativity. In the movie industry, they have the stamina to work the long hours of film shooting, but their need for stability doesn't make them the best candidates for living with the roller coaster cycle of going long periods without work or a paycheck. While working as a movie extra in Hollywood, many production personnel I met had 4 Birthdays. Production people work with the nuts and bolts end of movies. As artists, they continue to be solid as rock and forceful, whether their medium be art, composing, writing, or some sort of performing art, as embodied in the intensive musical style of Richard Wagner whose works are the basis for the cliché "Wagnerian Opera," meaning forceful and dramatic and the actor/director, Clint Eastwood. He is known for providing a strong screen presence, but his only Academy Awards have been for behind the camera work for the movies **Bird** and **The Unforgiven**. 4s always bring a steadfast nature to any movie or television role. Clint Eastwood is most famous for his typically rock solid, no nonsense acting style

Jack Nicholson is another critically acclaimed 4 Birthday whose basic mode of acting never changes. His style has not changed and is in constant demand because of his consistent steadfast style and deadpan humor. Robert Stack, from the 1960 series **The Untouchables** and the television documentary/drama series, **Unsolved Mysteries**, stared straight at the camera and talked about everything from UFOs and reunited families to kidnapping, bank robberies, and martyrs with the same poker face expression. When I saw a photo of him smiling, I thought it had been altered for public relations reasons. In the opening scene of the television series that carried his name, deadpan comedian Dick Van Dyke tripped over the ottoman in the middle of the room and immediately got up and acted as though nothing had happened. He jumped around the ottoman later in the series. This probably was his way of telling everyone he never was comfortable in his comedy role. Van Dyke never had another television series, but the style of comedy he and the program created have been an inspiration to American comics, and since then his contribution to entertainment has been through his own production company.

A 4 Birthday actor does best at what is known as a "character actor," someone with a consistent style. In the same vein, impressionistic art may have been a radical departure from the traditional school of artistic thought, but the impressionists were very softly stubborn about their right to be out of the mainstream of creativity. Is it any wonder that many impressionists were 4 Birthdays? The impressionistic movement was a cultural revolution.

Many 4s have great intuitive potential, but they're solid way of thinking gets in the way and sometimes causes those to doubt their intuitive ability with all this pent-up energy, 4s are stressful by nature. The 4's very hard emotional nature and strong physical inclinations extend into personal relationships and romance and makes them appear the hard-noses of the world.

A homebody tendency makes a 4 woman a good homemaker. 4s are at the forefront of those who have difficulty showing their gentler side because it is easier for them to scream than cry. A 4's need for order and well defined boundaries can cause the female to worry about her looks and aging no matter how attractive she is because she cannot control time. They can easily assume a brick wall persona and need to make sure they don't create their own emotional prison. Clint Eastwood did a wonderful job in **The Unforgiven**, but he definitely had a problem with the crying scene. Jack Nicholson also had done little crying in the movies, and the one thing that comes to mind is the one in **Five Easy Pieces** between Jonathan and his father. Nicholson cried but with much reserve. In the realm of intimacy, they prefer, even need, to be in control. They do not trust easily in either business or personal relationships. The old joke, "in God we trust, all others pay cash," expresses the 4's attitude in business until he knows you better. An emotionally balanced 4 is among the most dependable of the numbers, however, an insecure 4 who is too concerned about keeping up with the status quo and can become a great liar.

Two 4 Birthdays in any close emotional or work relationship need to have well defined boundaries and spheres of influence, less they get into ongoing power struggles and emotional combat. A 1/4 marriage is both emotionally and physically dynamic but control would be an ongoing issue. A steadfast 4 man would want the female 1 to be there for him more and she might oblige to make him happy. The female 1 also would be more outgoing and her 4 Birthday husband would have no problem turning into a couch potato, however, a 1 Birthday man could remain aloof and the 4 woman would be a good homemaker.

In a 2/4 relationship, it wouldn't take a psychic to figure out who would be in control, especially if the 4 is a man. This could be a marriage made in heaven if the woman craves someone who truly is in control of her environment and personal finances, or it could become a self-addressed invitation to a concentration camp.

Of the possible 3/4 combinations, a 4 and a 21 Birthday might find common ground, also much healthy friction, and they are equally fixed natures. If the 3 is a woman, she would be the man's mental match. If the 4 is a woman, she would want him to be more serious.

Chapter 18: Maturity Number

Your maturity number refers to the later part of your life and describes how your personality develops. As you grow more mature it becomes stronger. It begins to emerge from about the age of thirty as you gain a better understanding of yourself. It is also called the reality or ultimate goal number.

To calculate your maturity number add your life path and destiny numbers together and reduce if necessary.

You're moving towards being fully independent. You will be active and in charge of many things. You could be set in your ways. Your challenge is to break free of dependence on others and avoid being self-centred.

You're moving towards re-evaluating your emotional sensitivity. You will find inner calm and a sense of balance. You possess a talent for understanding and working with other people. Your ability to influence others will grow and your talents help to further you in your career. Your challenge is to avoid being insensitive or a doormat.

You're moving towards enjoying your creative abilities. Your later years will be filled with friends, creativity and fun. You become more extrovert and optimistic. Your later years will be fun-filled and you may take up an artistic hobby, such as playing a musical instrument. Your popularity will increase. Your challenge is to avoid superficiality.

You're moving towards enjoying the fruits of your labours. You will be able to better understand your limitations and can up with practical goals. You are less willing to cut corners and are approaching a time of accomplishment. Your challenge is to embrace your faults and avoid being narrow-minded or opinionated.

You're moving towards being more flexible. You will start serious travelling and become more dynamic and versatile, beginning to realise your lifelong goal of freedom. Your originality, creativity, and verbal abilities grow stronger. Your challenge is to avoid impatience and becoming bored.

You're moving towards being more concerned with the well-being of friends and family. You offer comfort and advice to those in need and become more responsible and protective. Your careful approach provides you with security later in life. Your challenge is to avoid being self-righteous and meddling in things that are none of your business.

You're moving towards spending more time in contemplation. You become more pre-occupied with the bigger questions in life and broaden your knowledge. Your intuition will improve. Your challenge is to avoid becoming isolated.

You're moving towards deepening your commitment to your work. You want people to be able to rely on you and you seek material success. You find it easier to overcome difficulties. You will be known for your common sense. Your challenge is to avoid becoming egotistic and obsessed with money.

You're moving towards being more selfless. You will devote your efforts to helping the less fortunate and grow to appreciate the arts more. Your challenge is to avoid becoming conceited.

You're moving towards improved intuition. You will help others realise their potential. Your challenge is to avoid a lack of motivation.

You're moving towards advising all those who call on you. You will be teaching and advising a wide range of people. Your challenge is resentment at not having enough time for yourself.

You're moving towards becoming a healer. This is extremely rare. Your powers of intuition and compassion will increase. Your challenge is to heal yourself before others.

KARMIC NUMBER

The karmic numbers are 13, 14, 16 and 19. When calculating your numbers you may arrive at 1, 4, 5 or 7 by combining double-digit numbers. When 4 is preceded by 13 or 5 by 14 a karmic debt is read as part of the interpretation. As 11, 22 and 33 stand on their own, always add an 11 as an 11, rather than a 2 (for example).

13-4 Transformation

You need to make up for a past of ignoring responsibility and refusing to do hard work. You have frittered away your talents and opportunities and will now be called on to learn discipline, vision, dedication and focus. You may often feel burdened and frustrated and want to simply give up. The key to success is focus. You need to maintain order and keep things under control.

14-5 Redress imbalances

Your debt revolves around the abuse of freedom and self-indulgence. You may have used others badly in the pursuit of freedom. You need to learn the lessons of discipline, integrity and commitment. You may be forced to adapt to circumstances and the unexpected. You need to learn flexibility and adaptability.

16-7 Epiphany

You have abused love in your past and hurt those around by refusing to acknowledge their needs. You can sometimes feel isolated and alone. You need to learn to think of others.

19-1 Harvest

You were in a position of power and used it without concern for those you harmed. You need to learn not to use others to suit your needs and stop blaming them for anything that goes wrong in your life.

Conclusion

It is just amazing how numbers can have a huge effect on our lives; I mean from the career path we need to follow to our life path and even to the goals we need to achieve. By simply knowing the meaning of your day of birth as well as your core number, you can use this knowledge to achieve greater things. You will thus not have the same predicament as many people who are unable to achieve their goals and ambitions because they are unaware of their innate abilities that can help them achieve those goals. However, with the information from this book, you now know what you are made of and you can use this knowledge to do many things

www.ingramcontent.com/pod-product-compliance
Lightning Source LLC
Chambersburg PA
CBHW072012070526
44583CB00015B/1450